3

Fulfilment

Fulfilment

Hans-Martin Barth

SCM PRESS LTD

Translated by John Bowden from the German
*Wie ein Segel sich entfalten: Selbstverwirklichung und
christliche Existenz,*
published by Christian Kaiser Verlag, Munich 1979

© Christian Kaiser Verlag, Munich 1979
English translation © John Bowden 1980

All rights reserved. No part of this publication
may be reproduced, stored in a retrieval system,
or transmitted, in any form or by any means,
electronic, mechanical, photocopying, recording
or otherwise, without the prior permission of the
publisher, SCM Press Ltd.

334 00524 8

First published in English 1980
by SCM Press Ltd
58 Bloomsbury Street, London WC1

Phototypeset by Input Typesetting Ltd, London
and printed in Great Britain by
Richard Clay (The Chaucer Press) Ltd
Bungay, Suffolk

Contents

Foreword

I mentioned to a friend who was staying with us that I was writing a book about fulfilment. He then told me the following story.

Once upon a time there was a farmer who found a large bird's egg in the woods. He took it home and had it hatched in his hen-house. Out of the egg emerged a bird which immediately began to imitate the hens, scratching and pecking in the yard as they did. One day the farmer was visited by a man who knew something about birds. He was rather surprised, and said to the farmer, 'Don't you know that the bird you're rearing out there is an eagle?' 'But it's scratching and pecking like my hens,' said the farmer. Some time later the man who knew about birds returned, and saw the eagle still in the farmyard. So he shouted out to it, 'You're an eagle, fly away!' Just for a moment, the eagle seemed to hear him, but then it turned its head away and went on scratching in the farmyard. The man who knew about birds came to the farmer for a third time and saw that the eagle was still there. So he took it out of the farmyard and carried it up a high mountain, from which there was a clear view of the sun. He spoke a few gentle words, and then – after a brief pause – the eagle spread its wings and soared into the air, towards the sun. . .

Why does anyone bother with what that story is all about?

Because of discovering an inner affinity with the eagle among the hens, with the farmer, or with the man who knew about birds?

Who reads books about fulfilment? Who writes them? Presumably those who do not want to take themselves and their life for granted; those with a marked awareness of themselves and the world around them; those with a strong sense of responsibility. They will be people who have been roused by something; something perhaps that has shaken them out of their acceptance of the greyness of everyday existence, has halted their headlong journey through the weeks and months of the working year, has even sent them off the rails. Perhaps they have had an accident, which has suddenly made the calendar and its terrors seem quite irrelevant; or a set-back in business or profession, which seems once and for all to have destroyed all optimism or pleasure in work; or friends or relations have been involved in a catastrophe which threatens the very will to live. People can also be aroused through a slow and constantly interrupted process, during the course of which it emerges that the passing of the years throws up certain questions, that limitations emerge which cannot be overcome. The problems of middle life begin; resources have to be sub-jected to careful scrutiny. What can I still do? Given favourable circumstances, what can I still achieve? And what should I put out of my mind for good?

It may also be that people read or write about fulfilment because they have been looking hard at the world around them. What does fulfilment mean for the fifteen-year-old in the process of growing away from the family? What does it mean for little Abdullah, who goes to a special school because he is not at home either in his mother tongue or in the language of his 'host country', and has to face a situation of increasingly harsh competition on the labour market? What does fulfilment mean in the face of manipulation by the media, in the fight against the powers of political structures and social institutions, before which the individual feels more and more helpless and exposed? A whole series of cumulative tendencies in our political, economic and cultural life seem to suppress the individual and attack human rights, rather than leading to a sense of worth, the possibility of development and the realization of potentialities. Those who see individuals threatened in this way, who want to try to help men and women who feel that they are being put through the shredder, will have to consider what fulfilment means and how it can be achieved. They will include the teacher dealing with pupils, the telephone Samaritan and the marriage counsellor, the leader of a youth group and the member of a relief organization of one kind or another. They will also include the mother scratching her head for some remarks which will help her growing children, or the person who sees a friend tangled up in a hopeless situation. We all ask, 'What are we really here for?' What possibilities do we have? How are we responsible for the existence that we have been given?

Many of the professional helpers and counsellors in our country, many of those who are concerned with the meaning of human life and what will be for the best, have been influenced by Christianity. What contribution can Christianity make towards human fulfilment? Some people may be unconsciously filled by a vague longing for a new spirituality, for a life-style which show us a meaningful way of living and the means of achieving it. People may also have romantic or nostalgic feelings, longings for an all-embracing pattern which will make sense of everything, in general and in particular, from the ringing of the alarm clock in the morning to the television news in the evening. However, though these longings may be given a Christian colouring, they seem to be evoked principally by humanist insights and questions which need to be taken seriously. Freud and Oedipus, Marx and Prometheus dog our footsteps. Those who have not been afraid to discover something about psychology and sociology will presumably have found how helpful they can be towards recognizing our own problems and understanding them better, finding helpful solutions and putting them into effect. The idea of fulfilment does not originally derive from the Christian tradition; it is much more of a humanist notion. If fulfilment and faith are not to be mutually exclusive, is not fulfilment something by which the believer sets least store, and faith something that can only hinder and impede fulfilment? The diaries of the Prior of Taizé, Roger Schutz, contain the observation that Christ did not ask people to 'Look for yourself' or 'Run after yourself', but to 'Come and follow me.' Schutz suspects that the man who furthers himself at the expense of others will puff himself up 'like a leech' and find that he is just pursuing a mirage.[1] Does not the sinful 'imagination of the thoughts of the human heart' (Gen. 6.5) appear in most concentrated form in the idea of fulfilment put forward by the humanities? Is not fulfilment the supreme embodiment of sin? Those involved in the dispute between pastoral care oriented on therapy and pastoral care with an evangelical slant are in fact fighting a battle for the whole of theology. It does seem as though the well-tried methods of secular humanism work better than the traditional pastoral approach which relies on the Bible, the hymn book and the confessional, even if they are only applied in dilettante fashion. Does that mean that the only function of the Christian tradition is to give the telephone Samaritan or the hospital visitor with a secular therapeutic training a bad conscience?

My experience so far and my theological reflections have convinced me that faith and fulfilment belong together, that Christian faith shows what fulfilment really is and that fulfilment is the way in which our faith is realized. To use an old-fashioned term from the history of Christian spirituality: for believers, fulfilment and 'sanctification', fulfilment and a life lived in faith are one and the same thing. If the believer understands his life as a Christian in terms of fulfilment, a fulfilment taking place within structures which can be elucidated by psychology or sociology, his faith will be 'fleshed out', will be rooted in and interpreted through reality. And if he sees fulfilment as a process which depends on faith and would be meaningless and even contradictory without it, he will discover for himself and others what Christian faith can mean for the enrichment of human existence. If there are readers who want to live as Christians but at the same time have their doubts about the humanities, let me encourage them to accept what the human sciences now say about the development and realization of human existence, and allow their faith to be expressed in a way which is grounded in reality. And if there are readers who see the Christian tradition as a threat and a danger to fulfilment as promised by psychology or sociology, let me remind them how easy it is to misunderstand a call to faith. Rightly understood, it can lead us towards fulfilment, and indeed can take us far beyond mere concern for ourselves. And if there are readers who feel pulled in both these directions, I hope that they will sustain the tension long enough to discover ways in which it can be made fruitful. Finally, I would like to say how helpful I personally have found my reflections on all these questions, not only theoretically but also in practice. I hope that they will prompt readers, too, to look for ways in which they can progress towards fulfilment.

Some people may find chapters 4 and 5 rather difficult: they are more specifically theological and necessarily somewhat abstract. If so, they will find that the going gets easier again in chapter 6, 'Fulfilment in Faith', or at the latest in the specific examples discussed in chapter 7. However, perhaps a theme which is of such immediate importance to our own lives will prove a stimulus towards following the theological argument and seeing how far it holds together!

1 Discovering Ourselves

... but who are we to ask about ourselves?

Joachim Illies

Who am I?

Suppose we begin from situations with which we are familiar. We have to introduce ourselves, to an individual or a group of people. So we give our name, say where we come from and what we do. Imperceptibly, saying who I am becomes a description of *what* I am (and allows me to demonstrate to myself where I work and what I have achieved). Details about family or even a professional title serve as shorthand explanations by means of which the person with whom we are talking can place us. If I only want to say enough to enable someone to carry on a conversation with me for an evening, or a limited period of time, then I may simply give my first name. (Students have tended to do this for years.) No address book or telephone directory will reveal where I live, with whom I live, or where I am to be found, unless I supply the information myself. There are a number of ways – some of them a necessary protection – of keeping back detailed information about who I am, but – do I know that myself? Perhaps I am applying for a job and have to provide a *curriculum vitae*. In that case I give my date and place of birth, my parents, my educational qualifications and my professional achievements, the length of my marriage and the number of my children. But does that describe who I am? Perhaps I could fill out this bare account with more detailed information and anecdotes, covering each period of my life, so that it becomes a thick volume of memoirs. But what would that say about the real me, about my hopes and disappointments? One can hear ridiculously long lists of personal achievements in funeral services; and also scant biographies, as though there were nothing at all to be said about some people. Born in Chipping Norton, died in Chipping Norton (and now buried in the churchyard at Chipping Norton). What is the real content of the space on the tombstone which separates the date of birth from the date of death? How does one fill in the details? Leaving aside the obvious facts, what has been the inner development of my life? What fulfilment have I found? What have I lost? Karl Jaspers tried to write a spiritual autobiography of this kind (he called it *Philosophische Autobiographie*) to explain the development of his thought. However, in this respect even thought seems too superficial. As Goethe's Werther puts it: 'Anyone can know what I know, but my heart is mine alone.' What is this heart, which has to be so 'alone'? What is expressed in the lines and folds on our faces? I read somewhere that by the age of sixty everyone is responsible for their facial appearance. Who am I? Who might I be? Who was I? Who should I be?

These questions are forced on us not only by the people around us or the anonymous society which imposes its norms on us. We get the impression that in the long run here is a problem which we cannot avoid, and that no psychological or sociological explanation of our situation will really satisfy us. The humanities can only give a limited answer to the question of human existence, because they arose out of this question and are themselves the embodiment of it. They can help to clarify the way in which human beings ask questions about themselves, the factors which shape their questioning and the aims they have in view. But they have to give up when it comes to the question why man is concerned about his nature and how he can be fulfilled. They cannot explain why he has developed a whole series of humane sciences, why he does not come to life unquestioningly, like a plant or an animal, and then disappear again. Men, too, may discover this unquestioning acceptance of being, when they are overwhelmed by the sight of the sea or a mountain range, a thunderstorm or a glorious dawn; when their whole being is taken up in the movement of a 'cello bow, or when lovers are together. But is this what we understand as identity, authentic life, the successful fulfilment of our selves? Are we satisfied with sinking into the universe, being caught up in the world around us, and in so doing losing our identity, renouncing any clear profile of ourselves? In our present circumstances, many of our contemporaries obviously find it attractive to use particular practices and techniques to produce this blissful feeling, which comes upon us so seldom of its own accord. However, no matter how much relief may be found here, we need to ask whether this is not to evade the call to be ourselves at the expense of being caught up in a greater whole, whether we are not succumbing to a creaturely need for security instead of boldly affirming ourselves and our calling in and to creation. It may be unfashionable to say so, but perhaps Yoga or Zen may be a retrograde step for Western man, moulded as he is by Christianity. Man as he is depicted in the Bible does not allow himself to be swallowed up in a consciousness which goes beyond being and non-being, but pays attention to the question, 'Adam, where are you?' Where are you hiding? Are you where you might be, where you should be? Are you where you may find some fulfilment? The question is a critical one; it brings uncertainty and leads to equivocation, projected as it is on to the God of Genesis, whose footsteps can be heard in the garden of Eden. No one can escape it completely; it crops up inexorably at one point or another, even if the portrayal of God as the inconvenient questioner seems an out-of-date way of putting things. And if this question has lost none of its truth and topicality, the same is true of another: 'Where is your brother Abel?' We experience the same feeling of inevitability when we are asked not only about ourselves, but also about our fellow men. In biblical terms, the modern question 'Who am I?' is split up into two other questions: 'Where are you?' and 'Where is your brother?'

Other ways of clarifying someone's identity appear in the Bible. In the Gospel of John, the origin of a man is his most important characteristic. 'Where are you from?', demands Pilate of Jesus when he is brought before him (John 19.9), and in the context of the gospel we sense that the question is concerned with more than Jesus' home town. 'Where do I come from?' is also a biblical way of asking, 'Who am I?' What is the ultimate foundation of my existence? What are the final norms for my action? Am I 'of the truth', 'of the light', 'from above' – or does my origin lie elsewhere?

Finally, there is a way in which the people of the Bible ask questions about themselves which is almost lost to us. They sometimes cry out in terror, 'Who am I that . . .?' They put this question in connection with quite specific situations and their demands: 'Who am I that I should go to Pharaoh?' Don't I have too high an opinion of myself? Isn't too much being asked of me? (Ex. 3.11). 'Who are you that you are afraid of man who dies?' (Isa. 51.12) – think about that and what you really need! Outsiders, too, can raise such questions: the people who came into contact

4

with Jesus began to ask: 'Who is this that he . . .?' (Luke 7.49; Mark 4.41). He makes a claim, he exercises authority – who is he? What is his secret?

Questions about ourselves involve a series of further questions. Who am I, where do I belong and what is my origin? Where is my brother? Do I know where he is? Am I looking for him in order to be a brother to him? Where do I come from? What governs my existence? Do I have the right idea, or do I have pretensions about what 'I am'?

Who might I be?

No matter who I am, I probably have some more or less clear idea about who I might be, or rather, who I might like to be, even if realization of my hopes lies somewhere in the future. I know what 'doesn't suit me'; I know the things that 'aren't really me': these phrases normally associated with fashion are by no means inappropriate here. We may not always be aware of the fact, but when someone suggests that we do something in particular, or when we are suddenly tempted, we know that there are some actions, some forms of behaviour which are alien to us. One part of human nature is evidently the question who we might be, who we should be, who we must be. 'Did you not know,' asked the twelve-year-old Jesus, disappointed at his parents' reaction, 'that I must be in my Father's house?' (Luke 3.49).

How can I discover who or where I 'must' be, in order to be myself and no one else? Furthermore, what is the explanation of this 'must', and what does one do about it? Earlier generations thought of a great universal law, a destiny which permeated the universe and determined the lives of individuals:

5

Formed by the day which saw you brought to birth,
by influence of planets, stars and sun,
you grow and go your way upon this earth
after the law by which it was begun.
'It must be thus, there can be no escape,'
so spoke the Sibyls, so the prophets told.
No time, no power can ever crush the shape
which in this ordered life starts to unfold.[2]

This 'primal, Orphic word' may not say everything, but
the basic attitude which it expresses is clear. Ancient belief
in the power of destiny, in the inexorable courses of the
stars, is combined with a view of the power of organic
nature, acquired as a result of science but given a religious
interpretation: who I may and must be emerges from what
I am. My personality has to develop in accordance with
pre-existing laws; the less interference there is with this
course of development, the more clearly my personality
will reach the heights of its potentiality. Present-day feelings evidently run in a different direction: those who con-
sult horoscopes are probably less concerned with fulfilment
than with the minutest pieces of good fortune which may
come their way. That is also why we do not talk of 'growth'
in this context. We can hardly understand our human
existence in the same terms as that of a plant, which blos-
soms at the appropriate time, and which requires comparatively little to fulfil the purpose for which it is intended.
All it has to do is to remain still in the ground in which it
has been planted, and wait for the sun and rain to play
their part. That is why, in human terms, we prefer to talk
of 'fulfilment'.

Unless I am mistaken, to talk of 'fulfilment' implies an
element of impatience, of activism, indeed of productivity.
We fulfil a plan, a programme. That presupposes that we

know what has to be done, and that reality lags a little behind our planning. However, the goal seems to be achieved, not by passively placing ourselves at the disposal of others, but by active intervention with a view to change. It is all up to me. Anything that I do not do well goes wrong; anything that I do not fulfil remains unfulfilled. Thus anxiety creeps in: if I do not fulfil myself, I will fall short of what I really am: I will remain unreal, inessential, inauthentic. I must realize myself in order to escape from the shadowy realm of the unreal, the void, nothingness, never having been, which could ultimately swallow me up. At least, that is our lurking suspicion.

How do we understand the 'self' in this context? From the start, the term 'fulfilment' seems to have a bias towards individualism or even narcissism. The use of the word 'self', and many of the compound words of which it forms a part, derives from the terminology of the sixteenth to eighteenth centuries, from a development in which the individual learnt to be articulate about himself over against his environment as he grappled with the demand thrust upon him to play a large number of different roles in an increasingly complicated society. What is generally understood by fulfilment can become an enormous burden, particularly to anyone who for any reason cannot or does not want to involve himself in a competitive situation. In some circumstances the very question of fulfilment can prove élitist and irresponsible. Those who write or read books about fulfilment would do well to remember that at this very moment countless people on our earth do not know where they can find a doctor or a hospital, or where they can learn the alphabet and the multiplication tables. What is fulfilment, as long as these elementary presuppositions for survival have not been ensured?

Just as the question of our authentic self can isolate us

from our environment, so the rest of the world around us can begin to fade once the limelight of our interest is turned on ourselves. On the other hand, we need our surroundings for landmarks, to provide a mirror in which we can recognize ourselves and see our profile. The Guatemalan author Augusto Monterroso has written a bitter satire which serves as a grotesque expression of the obscure relationship between the self and its environment, along with its dire consequences. It is the story of the frog who wanted to be a proper frog.

First of all he brought himself a mirror, and kept looking into it to see if he could discover his innermost self in it. . . Later he tried to find his true worth mirrored in the eyes of others. He preened himself, took the greatest care over his toilet, and in every respect tried to present himself as the model frog. He soon discovered that people prized his body most, particularly his legs, so to universal approval he prescribed for himself a course in hopping and jumping, to develop his thighs.

Last of all, simply to be regarded as a proper frog, he even allowed his legs to be torn off. Bitterly he heard the conversation at the subsequent meal: 'What splendid frog! Almost like chicken!'[3]

Who might I be? Perhaps to begin with I am aware of one particular capacity that I would like to develop. Perhaps I have a need to assert myself against an environment that gets in my way. Or I want to achieve something, realize something – and am afraid of failure, afraid that I might not live up to my own demands or those of my surroundings. I might even be eaten up by all these expectations and demands. The frog may have gone about things in quite the wrong way, but the question remains. Who might I be – 'a proper person', 'truly myself'? I cannot

8

evade the question who I might be. Flowers open in accordance with a predetermined plan, but man is challenged by the question how and whether he will open, and what it is that is blossoming' What is up with us? 'I do not understand my own actions. For I do not do what I want, but I do the very thing I hate . . . I can will what is right, but I cannot do it' (Rom. 7.15ff.).

Authentic people

When we begin to ask about our own fulfilment, people automatically come to mind who in some respects have reached the goal to which we aspire, and others who have fallen short of it. It makes sense for us to keep in mind the influences which determine our secret and our acknowledged ambitions: figures which belong to the landscape of our childhood and from there exercise a tacit influence on us: friends or colleagues, or perhaps also people with whom we did not get on very well and who yet seem to us to have been authentic. I am reminded here particularly of an old Protestant clergyman in a market town in southern Germany. There was something comical about him, with his inevitable black suit and the lace round his old-fashioned collar; there was an element of cunning in his dry way of telling humorous anecdotes and commenting on the day's events. He was unmarried, and lived for his calling; he took services and visited the sick, was available to anyone who might knock at his door, and would stop on the street at any time for a brief conversation. I once saw him in the midst of the hectic turmoil of a large city station; he even had a few friendly words for the clerk in the ticket office. Along with his sister he kept open house, and there were always longer-term guests of one kind or another who might stay for weeks, if not months: theological students who had failed their examinations, exiles, foreigners. His study was like that of a baroque scholar, and in the morning he would stand at his prayer desk, head sunk in prayer. He had a regular and disciplined prayer life; every day he would meditate (as we would now say) on a section of Luther's Little Catechism – 'I'm working through it,' he used to say. He read a psalm each day, and when he had come to the end of the Psalter in Hebrew he would read it in Greek, and then in Latin, before beginning all over again with the original text. He always seemed to have time, and I suppose that in the course of his life he did not do much that he did not really want to do. Some of the things that he wanted to do might seem questionable in another context, but hardly any of those who knew him would dispute that he did what he felt to be important, that he tried to live what he believed. For me he has always been the embodiment of a man for whom fulfilment and Christian existence were one and the same thing, and as a result was able to exercise considerable influence on his surroundings. I have kept meeting such people, not just old men, but people of my own age and younger. I can think of a colleague who can tell me with bright and sparkling eyes, and without even a suggestion of defensiveness, what he hopes for, what his ambition is and what he needs to realize it. I do not always agree with the substance of his ideals, but I find both him and what he says authentic.

I try to imagine what it might be like never to have had any encounters of this kind. I suppose that in former times the legends about the saints had this function of depicting authentic life and providing an introduction to it. Francis of Assisi may seem to have been somewhat mad in his argument with his furious father, his voluptuous praise of poverty and his conversation with the birds. Be this as it may, he helped his longing to break through, he did not

10

stifle the songs which uplifted him, and with utter consistency he chose the kind of life that he knew would fulfil him.

No weary soul was he, with downcast eyes
and face with furrowed brow and lines of care;
among the meadows lit by smiling skies
he'd greet the flowers like brothers, talking there
of life and love, and how he'd ever strive
to make the world a place of boundless joy.
His heart was warm and throbbingly alive,
and nothing could his peace and calm destroy.
He came from light, with yet more brilliant light,
his cell bathed with a happy, radiant glow,
while smiles and laughter flourished in his sight. . .[4]

Perhaps we might prefer to think of more 'modern' saints – Albert Schweitzer, Dag Hammarskjöld or Mahatma Gandhi. Was not Gandhi, too, an authentic man, one who fulfilled himself? He entitled his autobiography *My Experiments with Truth*. How do we recognize authentic people? There is also a negative authenticity, a criminal authenticity. There are people in whom the good does not seem to combat evil in any way, who have no scruples about acting wickedly, who 'watch to do evil' (Isa. 29.20).

What are we to make of the authenticity of the demonic and its most expressive representatives?

A purely formal principle of authenticity, a seamless, effortless correspondence between what we want and what we achieve, is evidently not enough for the fulfilment towards which men look. Otherwise fulfilment would be no more than the unfolding of a law within us, the kind of development that we may also observe in plants or animals. People may occasionally envy trees – yet anything that could fulfil itself in that way would not be a person. We are not presented with authenticity as an unproblematical form into which we need only grow – uncertainty and inability to solve the question of our authenticity are an intrinsic part of this authenticity: people who seem to us, to all outward appearances, to be authentic, by no means regard themselves as at rest, having arrived at their goal. We evidently waver to and fro between two states which Dorothee Sölle has described as 'the wish to be ourselves completely' and 'the right to become another'.[5] Our fulfilment is evidently based on the possibility that we can change. Whether we succeed in fulfilling ourselves is bound up with the perspective within which we seek ourselves. It therefore seems appropriate to discover and take into account the different aims which are appropriate to human beings and the perspectives which individuals have adopted.

2 *Ideas of Fulfilment*

Then a longing seized me to explore my long-buried life.
Ernst Herhaus

Programmes for living

Perhaps Hermann Hesse should be mentioned first among
the modern authors who have been especially concerned
with the problem of fulfilment. His early stories, in particular, are full of figures who in more or less adventurous
ways break out of the middle-class society which they feel
to be inauthentic and untrue. Like Friedrich Klein, the
civil servant absconding to the south, they want to take
over control of their lives, 'knocking any other driver off
the seat with mocking laughter, and even if the vehicle
thereafter acted capriciously, drove over sidewalks or into
houses and people'. As Klein dreamed, 'it was still a deli-
cious thing to do and far better than being sheltered and
riding under the tutelage of others, remaining a child for-
ever'. At last to stop doing 'only what comes from others,
only things I'd learned, only good and proper things'; no
longer to live 'in the darkness and self-oblivion, pursuing
some kind of purpose, some duty, some plan', but rather
to learn from Teresina the dancer, 'the joy of a healthy
person in himself, the intensification of this joy into love
for another, belief in and acceptance of one's own nature,
trustful yielding to the wishes, dreams and games of the
heart.' She had 'the key to paradise': 'When you dance,

13

Teresina, and at many other moments too, you're like a tree or a mountain or an animal, or like a star, altogether alone, altogether by yourself. You don't want to be anything different from what you are, whether good or bad.' No matter where it might lead, to life or to one's own freely chosen death, only one thing mattered: to abandon oneself, 'And whoever had once surrendered himself, one single time; whoever had practised that great act of confidence and entrusted himself to fate, was liberated. He no longer obeyed the laws of earth; he had fallen into space and swung along in the dance of the constellations.'[6]

These words express, decades earlier, the great longing of a whole generation of drop-outs, of hippies, of drug addicts and members of communes with romantic ideals. There is good reason why the last years have seen a reawakening of interest in Hermann Hesse. His programme is one of life, helping life to break through, entrusting oneself to the universe, finding room for the elemental desires within. The more reflective among us may find somewhat naive such trust in a 'destiny' which is not defined more clearly, in the all-embracing process of the life which pulsates on all sides; the smooth transition from fulfilment to self-surrender may seem terrifying, and the political consequences of the 'solution' approved of here may be intolerable. Nevertheless, Hesse's characters present a valid expression of the longing for an authentic life free from distortion and alienation: achieving authentic life in harmony with the meaning of all life, like an effortless dance!

We hear a comparatively less romantic, more matter-of-fact and realistic-sounding proposal for fulfilment from the Marxist camp: the formation of the 'socialist personality, mature in every respect'. This notion begins from the connection between individual and society; as Marx argued

14

against Feuerbach, in his individual reality man is 'the totality of social relationships'. A Soviet Marxist describes it like this: 'Social relationships assume their individual form in the personality.'[7] In socialism, however, the theory runs, the difference between social and individual interests disappears; at the same time, 'as a result of the enrichment of social contacts and personal relationships, and through the increase of their spiritual wealth and the development of their talents, each individuality differs from all others and gains originality and character'. This is achieved through conflict, in active involvement in the collective, the society, which is represented by the personality of the individual. Thus we find the following statement in the programme of the Soviet Communist party for 1961: 'The new man is formed through his active participation in the building up of Communism, through the development of Communist principles in economic and social life, and under the influence of the whole educational system of the party, the state and the social organization. . .'[8] For the non-Marxist, too much emphasis may seem to be laid on the importance of society and its institutions; he may be diverted again and again from the theory to the practice of Communism in socialist countries today. Nevertheless, here too a great longing is expressed, the longing for a situation in which individual needs for an authentic, meaningful life no longer get in the way of one another, but supplement and enrich one another and together take wing. Here is the desire that one day a man's self need not have to seek fulfilment at the expense of another, nor one class to the detriment of another. The motto of this longing is, 'Act, and act together!' The best way for the individual self to shape and develop itself is in shared sacrifice.

Erich Fromm has introduced a third formula into the debate, which is also concerned with fulfilment: 'Be' instead of 'Have'! He observes that man, especially in Western society, experiences himself and his environment more in the mode of having than in that of being. Man does not seem to attach any real significance to anything that he does not possess. He has to pluck the rose, own the work of art, give his memory permanence in the form of films and photographs, support his conversation with facts; finally, he has his own dentist and his own particular medical complaint: he defines himself by his possessions. His environment defines him in the same way. What he is is not important; the vital thing is the particular knowledge and skill at his command. He sees that he is someone with a particular market value. He has to sell himself well. Finally, he even comes to feel that his ego is something that he has: 'The subject is not myself but *I am what I have. My possessions constitute me and my identity.*' Fromm contrasts this with the 'mode of existence': I should understand myself as a living process; I should learn to establish living relationships with my surroundings and no longer seize and manipulate them as a dead thing. My ego no longer stands and falls with what I possess or lose; I abandon myself to a living relationship with my partners, without having to protect or defend anything. From this perspective Jesus appears as 'the one who did not want to *have* anything', as the 'hero of being, of giving, of sharing'. What are the characteristics of the new man envisaged here?

Willingness to give up all forms of having, in order to fully *be*.

Security, sense of identity, and confidence based on faith in what one *is*, on one's need for relatedness, interest, love, solidarity with the world around one . . .

16

Developing one's capacity for love, together with one's capacity for critical, unsentimental thought . . .

Happiness in the process of ever-growing aliveness, . . . for living as fully as one can is so satisfactory that the concern for what one might or might not attain has little chance to develop.

This picture of a new man would be matched by a new society, the 'city of being'.[9]

Of course it may not be possible to distinguish being and having quite so neatly as is done here (especially for the have-nots). The analysis of the way in which men have fallen victim to the temptation of having, instead of being satisfied with being, may remain an unsatisfying one. Nevertheless, this programme presents a real possibility which anyone can try out and which many people today have clearly found helpful: breaking the spell of a great many alienations, coming to oneself, being!

The programmes for living presented to those in search of fulfilment can quickly be seen to be right, and equally quickly be seen to have limitations. Hermann Hesse's passionate summons to life appeals to us to the degree that we are prevented from living authentically by conventions, by the pressure exerted on us by occupation, family or background. But what is life when it might just as well be death, the intoxication of voluntary death and fervent sacrifice of life at the expense of others? The solemn Marxist conviction that the new man will be formed in a new society, that the individual finds fulfilment in active involvement on behalf of others, appeals to us in that we know that man cannot find his goal in a private happiness apart from his fellow human beings. But how can the individual protect himself and society from the operations of sheer power, working under the garb of an idea which sounds fine in theory, but

17

which exploits and misuses the life of the individual? We find Erich Fromm's matter-of-fact reference to the creative possibilities of being illuminating, to the degree that we feel the victims of commercial exploitation down to the most intimate part of our lives, to the degree that we see our intimations and our dreams die under the terror of competition and the pressure to achieve something. But is being a man not perhaps rather more than deliberately allowing oneself for a while to be carried along by the power of life? What is 'being' in the face of what we owe to one another, in view of the fact that we suffer, that at any time death can put an end – and one day will put an end – to our being and the being of those with whom we share creative relationships?

Christianity, too, puts forward a proposal for human fulfilment. 'Believe!' Might it not go further towards helping man to an appropriate, deeper fulfilment than the slogans 'Live', 'Sacrifice yourself', 'Be'?

Psychological and sociological aspects

There is a good deal of argument about the term 'fulfilment' in contemporary psychology. True, the 'orientation' of a living organism is generally recognized; but that does not amount to approval of religious or metaphysical theories which are incapable of empirical verification. Moreover, psychology has come into being as a result of the observation and the care of sick people in particular. From this perspective, man's primary concern seems to be not the achievement of a goal in life, but simply homoeostasis, the recovery of psychological balance.

Still, one group of psychologists – often classified under the title 'humanistic psychology' – think that the sick man cannot properly serve as a starting point. Even for these,

homoeostasis is possibly to be regarded only as an inter-
mediate stage. For them, man is concerned with 'self-
actualization', with 'growth', with the 'meaning' of his
existence, with 'self-realization' and 'fulfilment'.[10] The psychologist Abraham Maslow establishes a hierarchy of
human needs, built up in successive stages. Once physio-
logical needs like hunger and thirst are seen to, the need
for security emerges, and later the need for dedication and
love; if these are met, the 'needs for esteem' appear: hope
for success and recognition, until finally the need for self-
realization can be fully acknowledged. Of course it goes
without saying that the transitions within the framework
of psychological development are blurred. Charlotte Bühler
tries to speak of fulfilment rather less schematically. She
too notes a series of needs: the satisfaction of psychological
and physical drives, adapting to one's own limitation, creative expansion, enjoyment of activities and maintaining
inner order. Not everyone finds their fulfilment in the process of self-realization, which Charlotte Bühler sees in the
fact that people feel fulfilled when they can realize their
best possible characteristics and capabilities, i.e. their best
potentialities.[11] The dubious point is whether the best possible self-realization for the individual also represents the
greatest possible happiness for those around him, as Karen
Horney supposes, or, to put it the other way round, in the
last resort whether the individual does not have to renounce
many aspects of his fulfilment in view of conditions as they
actually are.

The fact that other people appear here primarily as
obstacles in the way of self-realization makes the difficulty
in this approach clear. Certainly it depends on the presuppositions of one's view of the world whether the accent is
put on the individual or society. However, it may be taken
for granted that self-realization can never be thought of

apart from the social context of the person in search of fulfilment, precisely because human individuality and human sociability should not be played off against each other, but condition and further each other. There are 'sociological dimensions of identity' (Lothar Krappmann); one only becomes oneself in human relationships (A. J. M. Vossen). Among the models which try to explain the reciprocal effects to be noted here, the proposal made by George H. Mead is particularly worth attention. He makes a distinction between 'I' and 'me'. The 'me' is formed in interaction with the world around, with expectations and demands made by the roles we have to play, whereas the 'I' is seen as the man who acts spontaneously and creatively, to the degree that he cannot be explained by his environment. Man, characterized by his own particular psychological and physical constitution, and with his unalterable biography determined by this constitution, comes up against the demands made by roles which change to an increasing degree. Now he must attempt to integrate all the various roles assigned to him; he has to see that they do not tear him apart and dismember him, so that he becomes an incredible marionette, made up of different limbs which do not match. On the other hand, he will have to seek to reconcile the existence characterized by a variety of roles with the subjective ego which he experiences as such. To take up an expression used by Jürgen Habermas, he has to see to a balance between his 'social' and his 'personal' identity.

Here we have touched on a broader perspective: the process of human individuation within which fulfilment is achieved, whether there is an attempt at its empirical investigation (Erikson), or whether it is sketched out transcendentally, along the lines taken by C. G. Jung, as a development directed towards maturity, the realization of possibilities and the acceptance of limitations. Fulfilment is unthinkable without its field of references, and without the history and development of the relationships which take place here.

When I examine the insights of psychologists and sociologists with a view to discovering the consequences that they may have for my own fulfilment, I discover four factors which I have to consider. Fulfilment can never be an abstract programme: the development has been going on for a long time even in those who are hearing the term for the first time. All conscious fulfilment is grounded in a more or less satisfying selfhood, probably a complicated process which has led to this particular make-up, the factors of which I should know. So I have to ask myself: what is my contribution to the physical and mental reality which I have probably taken over from my father or mother? Those of us who are fathers and mothers ourselves will hardly be able to escape noticing that much of what we have felt to be our innermost selves is evidently just passing through us – from grandparents to grandchildren. As parents, it is just chance that we stand in between as mere intermediaries. And yet we ourselves live out this alien, borrowed reality as our own. How do we deal with it? How much does it matter to us that we are short or tall, slight or imposing? That we are clumsy or volatile, gifted, clever and industrious, or that we have to work very hard because we have no natural gifts? Looking at our parents and ancestors, can we explain to ourselves why we rush after new things or stick to the old, why we find it difficult to make contacts or tolerate opposition?

When we reflect on these questions, our attention will soon be drawn to our personal history, the development of our bodies and minds over the whole period since we became conscious of them. Does our particular time of life explain why we are the way we are, or why we want to be different? Are we seized with some kind of panic at the possibility of being excluded, anxiety that we may fall short of or fail to live up to certain demands? Do we have a hidden longing for days past or days to come?

Finally, we shall be reminded of experiences of acceptance and rejection, security and threat. And conversely, we may ask, When have I made people happy, and when have I disappointed them? How will I cope with my failure and my success? What are my limitations? What are the personal or occupational complications in which I am involved? We need not understand characteristics of our psychological make-up, our history and our environment, simply, or even primarily, as limits on our possibility of fulfilment: the factors that seem to constrain us at the same time constitute our being. An abstract, idealized self that we might dream up would still have traces of our particular nature, our own previous experience, and the more strongly it diverged from that, the less we would be in a position to aspire to it as a realization of ourself. We do not achieve fulfilment by attempting to do away with what seem to be our limitations, but in some circumstances by grappling with them. We need the presuppositions which we bring with us and which seem to restrict us so much as the material from which, or even against which, we find fulfilment. But how do we find criteria here?

Even while we are attempting to take up a provisional position, there will be some things that we will be very ready to recognize and others that will be less welcome, which confront us with an urgent need to overcome particular characteristics or even to change them. Why is this? Once people begin to ask about themselves, their history and their environment, a further question cannot be excluded – which is in fact communicated by means of

22

these factors. What is the ultimate horizon of meaning? To answer it with a hasty reference to paternal authority and the problems of the super-ego seems to me to be superficial. For all the efforts so far made, an attempt to derive it from the first three factors and to identify it exhaustively with them has not proved successful. This is the question of the man who sees himself in the centre of the life which he perceives, and who must nevertheless move out of the centre, become 'ec-centric', if he is to see himself in such a way (H. Plessner). He loses his balance if he goes forward into nothingness without being aware of any horizon.

Taking psychological and sociological factors into account, then, I would describe 'fulfilment' in this way. It represents man's attempt to shape his own existence responsibly, i.e. against the background of an ultimate horizon of meaning, in the context of a social system of reference and at the particular stage of his existence which he has reached. Factors which would hinder fulfilment described in these terms would be a damaged relationship between the individual and his social surroundings, disruptive factors with regard to the stage of individuation which he had reached (Erikson) or within his individual process of maturing (Jung); but these would also prove a hindrance if horizons of meaning did not develop further in the course of the process of individuation or socialization and took on a threatening and finally constricting life of their own.

Some Christian dogmatic statements and many Christian moral judgments give rise to the suspicion that the horizon of meaning presented in Christian faith could be a decisive disruptive factor for the kind of fulfilment sought by psychology and sociology. Anyone who wants to reconcile fulfilment and Christian existence must take account of this objection.

23

3 *Christianity and Loss of Self*

> O Lord, take me away from myself
> and give me wholly to thee!
>
> *Nikolaus von der Flüe*

The accusation

That Christian belief is more of a hindrance than a help to
man's natural will to affirm himself and find fulfilment is
a claim which has found an ongoing series of proponents,
at the latest from the time of Nietzsche onwards – and is
shared by a large number of Christians.

> Christianity . . . has made an ideal out *opposition* to the
> preservative instincts of strong life.

> A certain sense of cruelty towards oneself and others is
> Christian . . . Hatred of *mind* . . . hatred of the *senses*, of
> the joy of the senses, of joy in general . . .[12]

Those who formulated the ideology of National Socialism
were able to take up this point and show how perverse and
inimical to nature the Christian notion of love must necessarily seem. With relish Alfred Rosenberg quoted the following remark: ' "Saint" Zeno said in the fourth century
AD: "The greatest boast of Christian virtue is that it tram-
ples nature under foot." The church faithfully followed this
principle wherever it was able to gain a footing.'[13] Decades
later, in his book of the same name, Karlheinz Deschner
lamented the 'cross with the church' and in conclusion

24

passed the following judgment on Christianity: 'It has not made people happier.' Above all in the sexual sphere: the Christian is regimented 'down to the innermost circuit of his brain and the last corner of his bed'. In essentials, he always lives in conflict with himself; in other words, he cannot live at all – fully, sensuously, without being broken apart – in an elemental way . . . He is not allowed to do what he really wants, and everything that he should do goes against his nature.' The church makes him fit for heaven and 'prepared' for the world.[14]

Now of course it could be said that these comments are reactions to exaggerations or even false developments in the history of Christianity; it is important to keep away from polemics. Or one could respond defiantly to the three critics. Yes, that is the Christian view of man; it is not really concerned with fulfilment, but with making people fit for earth and 'prepared' for heaven.

First of all, as a Christian, I am affected by this amount of disillusionment about Christianity. And I am reminded of one of my acquaintances who in a telling aside said that he felt cheated of his youth because at that time he still 'believed'. How could so much disappointment and mis-understanding arise – or is this the point at which in fact paths diverge: one goes to church and the other finds 'fulfilment'?

Fateful texts

A series of biblical texts seems to support this view: 'Whoever would save his life will lose it,' says Jesus (Mark 8.35). Of course this insight is still at a level at which we can comprehend it, and it plays a role in all religions. A Jewish rabbi once said: 'What should man do to live? He should kill himself! And what should a man do to die? He should be concerned about his prosperity.' Similar insights could be arrived at within the framework of the most varied religious and philosophical conceptions.

> Who knows if life be not death,
> and death life?

Hinduism and Buddhism also take similar insights for granted.[15] It dawns on us, we find confirmation from our experience, that life can become deeper and fuller as a result of renunciation, involvement and sacrifice. We accept a degree of limitation in our lives when this promises to contribute towards a heightening of our sense of living. Something of 'death' can prove to be a refined way towards more intensive life.

Christianity was necessarily moulded by biblical statements about asceticism, which were in fact confirmed by experiences of human religious self-awareness and to some degree are even also endorsed by modern psychological insights. Anyone who would become my disciple, Jesus said, must deny himself, take up his cross and follow me. 'Self-denial' becomes an independent course of action: one theological lexicon translates the corresponding Greek phrase 'act in a wholly selfless manner, give up his personality'.[16] Denying oneself means regarding oneself as completely unimportant, indeed as non-existent, but as a result also being free from anxiety about oneself, from everyday frustrations and oppressive dependent relationships. An impressive ideal, but one which in principle can be (and is!) realized in every religion, and which does not have much to do with specifically Christian faith. By contrast, the self-denial that Jesus means and requires is not an end in itself, which in the last resort also unleashes feelings of superiority; it is, rather, an obvious concomitant experience for anyone who become a disciple. Dietrich Bonhoeffer interprets it in this way: 'To deny oneself is to be aware only of Christ, and no more of self; to see only him who goes before and no more the road which is too hard for us.'[17] All the other biblical statements which point in this direction must also be seen from this perspective. 'Go, sell what you have, and give it to the poor . . . and come, follow me' (Mark 10.21). 'If your eye causes you to sin, pluck it out and throw it from you' (Matt. 18.9) – given the kingdom of heaven, it does not matter much whether you have one eye or two. Jesus says that if anyone comes to him 'and does not hate his own father and mother and wife and children and brothers and sisters, yes, and even his own life, he cannot be my disciple' (Luke 14.26). Of course, 'hate' here may be translated 'love less than', following the Semitic usage: the saying is primarily concerned with the relationship of a disciple to Jesus, which is so important that it makes all other relationships in which a man may be involved relative, and indeed can abolish them alto-gether. 'Christ has cut us off from all immediacy with the things of this world' – no man is in immediacy to Christ.[18] What we have here is the claim of Jesus and not a particu-lar religious ideal. Jesus was obviously sceptical about all religious ideals; otherwise he could hardly have been taunted as a 'glutton and winebibber' (Matt. 11.19). People interpreting the double commandment to love have sometimes wondered whether it might not nevertheless contain a hidden invitation to self-love and self-assertion. You must love your neighbour 'as yourself' – does that also mean 'myself'? In a hymnbook dating from the Enlightenment we find these guileless lines:

It is thy will, O God,
that I myself should love;
O grant that such a faith

27

my conduct sure may prove . . .

Now one can describe man's relationship to himself as 'love' only if one uses the word 'love' in an inauthentic sense. Furthermore, the phrase 'as yourself' is probably best interpreted in terms of the parallel formulation, 'with all your heart and all your soul and all your mind'. What is being discussed here is not man's relationship to himself but his relationship to God, to his neighbour and to his enemy. The great commandment, obedience to which would at the same time mean life and fulfilment, is that we should be devoted to God and our neighbour in all phases of our existence, with all our capabilities and all our will. Both consciously and subconsciously we should live unreservedly for God and our fellow men. Whether as a result of this basic attitude, which occupies us completely and utterly, we involve or withhold some of our capabilities, withdraw or develop some elements of our personality, is a secondary question to be decided in each specific situation.

If we go through the corresponding Pauline passages which at first sight seem to tell against self-affirmation and fulfilment, we arrive at the same result. Of course we 'are always sinners', but in the same breath Paul continues: 'and are justified by his grace as a gift, through the redemption which is in Christ Jesus' (Rom. 3.23f.). The Protestant Christian in particular has the passage from Romans 7 deeply stamped on his consciousness: 'For I do not do the good I want, but the evil I do not want is what I do.' But Paul concludes with the cry, 'Who will deliver me from this body of death? Thanks be to God through Jesus Christ our Lord' (Rom. 7.14–25). These are the words of a man who can breathe a sigh of relief and give thanks, although he feels divided in himself and incapable.

How was it possible that only one side of things, the negative one, inessential and obsolete, could fix itself in the consciousness of many Christians, so that self-disgust and the continual endorsement of feelings of inferiority succeeded in displacing the assurance of a new, happy and confident existence grounded in Jesus Christ? Even what is said about the dying of the old man and putting to death the deeds of the body (Rom. 6.3f.; 8.13f.) is qualified by the expectation of liberated, new, authentic life. Only when such talk is isolated from that expectation can it be reforged into an argument against the self-affirmation and the fulfilment of the Christian.

The clearest permanent corrective to such a false estimation is Jesus himself. Jesus did not enter the Christian consciousness as the great ascetic, the pattern and model of self-denial, detachment from the world and from oneself, but as the one who took God and man utterly seriously and whose apparent failure did not lead to a loss of identity, but to final fulfilment.

Piety at the expense of the self

Although texts of this kind served as a theological foundation for monasticism in the early church, the history of interpretation has largely preserved the dialectic between self-sacrifice and fulfilment. For example, Basil the Great, who is regarded as one of the fathers of monasticism, understands 'tearing away the soul' from its dependence on the body and the world as a 'preparation of the heart', which serves to bring more profound happiness and fulfilment. Above all in the wake of Neo-Platonism and mysticism, this dialectic threatened to take on independent form as a fact which could be demonstrated by psychology. It was thought to be an achievement to have come to terms

29

with this dialectic, and people almost lost sight of Jesus' call to discipleship. 'Knowing only Christ' and forgetting oneself became a self-sufficiency which asks for and desires nothing more. Everything that is called 'this and that', we read in the sermons of Meister Eckhart, must vanish from the heart; neither love nor sorrow may touch it any longer. The mystic will not object even if God's will should send him to hell. Though to begin with the Reformers were impressed by such arguments, they sensed behind them a subtle mechanism which could lead, precisely through self-denial, and indeed through the resolution of the tension between self-affirmation and self-denial, to an excessive emphasis on the self. Formally speaking, man might be concerned with God's glory, but this is the glory of a God understood in the philosophical or psychological conceptuality of neo-Platonism, an honour which should not be accorded to the God of Jesus Christ and his cross. Even the mystical 'self-sufficiency', which was surely one of the best elements of medieval piety, could surreptitiously be transformed into a religious 'work'. Luther, who of course did not sufficiently take into account that this need not necessarily be the case, attempted to go one stage further in his thinking: the man who may be certain of God's concern is not the one who surrenders himself piously, renounces everything and resolves the tension between 'nothing' and 'everything', but the person who despairs of himself.

Luther finds that self-denial is not a renunciation of this thing or that: 'No, you yourself should be done to death and become as nothing, holding back nothing in which you could still trust before God . . . God cannot but be other than gracious through Christ to anyone who despairs of himself in this way, and will give him all good things.'[19] Luther, still in the throes of mysticism, puts things somewhat obscurely, as though it were for God to be gracious to man: however, it is clear that man's negation is not an end in itself, but the indispensable presupposition of the saving intervention of God. Even the pietistic interpretation which, prompted by the continuation of mystical undercurrents, often reduces the encounter of man and God to the formula 'nothing' and 'everything', is concerned with *both* these things, 'that *man is nothing* and *God is everything*'.[20] Christian faith does not seek to deprive man of his honour and worth, but to show him how, free from anxiety about asserting himself and from consuming concern for his own self, as a reborn person and a new creation, he can find his 'everything', his authenticity and his true and abiding reality. It is God's 'everything' that is realized in man's 'nothingness'. But when this 'nothingness' of man becomes isolated from the care of God which offers him 'everything' and holds him in its grasp, when man is considered as a sinner without being thought of as surrounded by grace, then the doctrine of sin begins to take on a disastrous life of its own and leads to a kind of caricature of Christianity, for which to a certain degree the history of Christian theology must be made responsible. In that case man seems to be characterized by 'love of self' and 'desire' (Augustine); 'pride' and 'rebellion' become central characteristics of the man who keeps himself apart from God (and also of the demons) – and instead of the grace of God, a doctrine of man's burden of sin emerges triumphant.

This situation can also be read out of the practice of Christian piety. Let me take just a few examples. It may seem terrifying that in his prayers Francis of Assisi heard the summons: 'Francis, if you are to know my will, you must despise and hate what you have hitherto loved and striven for in the flesh.' Yet it can hardly be denied that Francis experienced this turning point in his life – exem-

31

plified in the kiss he gave to the leper – as an act of liberation, matched by his instructions to his brothers 'to be cheerful and lovable, as befits men who rejoice in their heart'.[21] Thus self-conquest and self-denial evidently always become dangerous when they become independent, when they are detached from service of God and man, when they threaten to become masochistically distorted means of self-satisfaction. When that has happened, the 'servant of God' has suddenly become no more than a 'servant', subject to some diffused superior power. In that case a confession like, 'I, I and my sins, which are like grains of sand on the sea shore', descends to being a scrupulous self-accusation instead of being a celebration of forgiveness and release from a burden; and in that case the amazed 'O God, how great you are' turns into the insipid children's prayer, 'I am small, make my heart pure', which can have disastrous effects once it becomes a ritual. This phenomenon may perhaps best be clarified by means of the well-known prayer of Nikolaus von der Flüe, which ends with the verse, 'O Lord take me away from myself and give me wholly to thee!' If my self-surrender ends in an ultimate sense of being accepted down to the very ground of my being, then my self is fulfilled. But if I remove the 'take me away from myself' from its context and interpret it in analogy with inter-personal dealings, it is reminiscent of political re-education, sadistic torture and brainwashing. In that case the therapist will soon be able to observe a series of 'church-derived neuroses' ranging from the ridiculous to the terrifying;[22] 'a big brother's face exercising constant control' opens its eyes, and an omnipresent 'figure which says no' begins to become oppressive.[23]

It is possible to suggest a number of reasons why such an isolation of the ascetic element in Christian belief could come about. First of all, it will have been nurtured by the practice of piety in Judaism; even in the New Testament we can see how the first Christians were put on the defensive because of their attitude to time-honoured practices like fasting (cf. Mark 2.18).

Asceticism also played an important role in the Hellenistic mystery cults, and in the last resort we may recall the hostility of Platonism and Neo-Platonism to the material world. But how could all this combine to get the better of Christianity and mould it right down to our century, in the eyes of its opponents and of many of its adherents? Perhaps the roots of this situation are more than historical. Perhaps the fact that Christian faith is misunderstood as a moral force, which cannot be harnessed without giving up a great many possibilities of self-fulfilment, is connected in an elemental way with this very need which man has to fulfil himself. Pelagius' doctrine of man's freedom for good and evil is more illuminating than Augustine's talk of the impossibility of not sinning; Kant's notion of duty finds acceptance more easily than Luther's insistence on Christ's cross and God's grace. Christian faith must do more than reject the charge that it hinders the development of the human ego while all the world is looking for fulfilment. Rather, it raises the counter-question: does not man himself, struggling for fulfilment apart from the gospel, introduce a great many programmes and techniques which diminish his own self? Theology calls this phenomenon 'sin'.

4   *Sin and Self*

The only thing that man may claim for himself is sin.
                                                        Karl Rahner

How can Christian faith talk about fulfilment and at the
same time maintain its views about the sinfulness of man?
It is certainly easy to demonstrate and to discover in practice that from an anthropological point of view, a doctrine
of sin which makes itself independent and as it were forgets
grace can and indeed must lead to disastrous consequences.
That makes all the more urgent the question whether this
is true only of an approach which takes sin in isolation, or
whether any talk of sin at all can be other than a disaster
for man.

When the Christian tradition talks about sin, it is more
concerned with sin as a qualification of actions and modes
of behaviour against which, if the 'market research' has
turned out all too negative, man must protest, as it were
because of the excessive demands being made on him. Sin
means more than transgressing a commandment, departing
from a norm or falling short of a goal. The 'sins' of which
one sometimes reads on cinema posters, or even 'sins
against the Highway Code', do not tell us anything about
what sin really is. The vague feeling that sin will probably
be something to do with attitudes towards our fellow men
remains in the foreground. 'Do not do to others what you
would not want to have done to yourself' would mean: I

look for fulfilment up to the point at which it begins to harm others; up to this point fulfilment is permissible, but beyond that it counts as sin. In that case, fulfilment would *a priori* involve a tendency to sin; for in the last resort, what does not harm my fellow-man? Above all, what would I not owe my neighbour were I to transpose the golden rule into the positive, as Jesus proposed (Matt. 7.12)? However, Christian talk about sin means more than objecting to particular human forms of behaviour; it contributes more than a demarcation between 'permissible' and 'impermissible', or the information that something is 'still within the limits of tolerance'. It refers not only to man's *action*, but rather to his *being*. It provides information not only about possibilities or limits of fulfilment, but above all about the self that seeks or should seek fulfilment. What is the relationship between sin and self? Over the course of the centuries, two types of answer have emerged in Christianity, which to some degree are reflected in the great Christian confessions.

The fight between sin and self

On the first pages of the Bible it is said that man was created 'in the image of God' and then 'fell'. A difficulty felt by theology at an early stage was the problem how it was possible to conceive of 'being in the image of God' and 'sin' at the same time. May man be regarded as God's image despite his sinfulness? Theologians responded with an artifice which they often used: they drew a distinction. At this point, Irenaeus taught, it is important to distinguish between 'being in the image of God' and 'being like God'. Likeness to God – understood in a moral sense – had been lost as a result of the Fall, but the image of God remained intact. In what might it consist? Whereas in the Western

35

tradition this image was primarily associated with human rationality and thus came to stand as an organ for perceiving the revelation of God's grace, the East continued to be more interested in the material orientation of the image of God, which was understood as a particular purposiveness established in man. In either case, part of man's self had not been attacked by sin; as Meister Eckhart could say, 'something in the soul' remained profoundly bound up with God. The basic structures of human existence had not been destroyed by sin; the house might be in ruins, but the foundations were still usable (we might illustrate the understanding of Eastern and mystical theologians by saying that the basement was still habitable). The important thing was to clear away the ruins and then build again on the intact basement. A scholastic motto was that grace does not destroy nature, but perfects it: the important thing, it was said at the end of the Middle Ages, is 'to do what is in one' – and this was in fact done, although it was often grotesque and superficial. At all events, sin and self were in no way to be identified: supported and preserved by God's grace, but at the same time confronting God as an independent being, the believer understood his self as something which was not hopelessly given over to sin, but could and had to fight against it.

Demonology may seem alien to us today, but it served as another way of differentiating sin and self. If a demon could be discovered who caused a man to sin, if Satan could be seen as the inspiration of the Fall, at any rate man did not have to take all the responsibility for sinning. He could excuse himself by appealing to the treacherous and overpowering might of the devil. Ivan Karamazov feels relieved when Aliyosha can assure him, 'You are not completely lost, you are not Satan himself.' The fact that Satan was not identical with man's own self was the basis for being able to fight against him, for being able to rebel against him. That is why the American pastoral psychologist, Seward Hiltner, Professor of 'Theology and Personality'(!), can understand New Testament demonology as a 'forerunner of the modern conception of psychological hygiene'.[24]

Now if it was possible to protect the self from identification with sin by references to God's good creation or to the supremacy of demons, what were the consequences for an understanding of 'fulfilment'? It could be said that a man should recognize the good foundations; make the most of his own potentialities, or allow them to be supplemented by God's grace; take up the struggle against evil; realize the good within him and develop it against all the incursions and threats of sin; put himself in the way of becoming a saint. The man who understood himself along the lines of this model could affirm one part of his reality, but he had to disown, fight against, suppress, and if possible blot out, another part of himself. Here asceticism was at the same time both an expedient and a partial goal. Nietzsche's judgment is exaggerated, but certainly very acute: 'In any ascetic morality, man worships part of himself as God and needs to turn the other part into a devil.'[25] This is the morality of the man who knows that he is neither beast nor angel, and that he has some good potentialities, if not the best, which it seems meaningful for him to realize. Here he is followed by our secular contemporaries, in their aims if not in their modes of expression. Fulfilment becomes the task of true humanity and the achievement of a strong personality.

The sin of self-alienation

In contrast to a Christian life-style which sought to arrive at human fulfilment with or without God's help, but at all events through an apparently pious course of action, the Reformers reflected on the biblical insights into the relationship between sin and self. With the best representatives of mediaeval piety, they were aware that man qualifies the action, and not the action the man. Luther thought that our infirmity lies 'not in works, but in nature'; if the tree were in order it would bring forth good fruits, and if the person were in better shape one would not have to ask so much about works. But what is the state of the person, the self?

This question must perplex anyone who is honest, because the same person puts the question, asks it about himself and gives the reply. It is a mark of human greatness that we can ask the question about ourselves at all, and it is our tragedy that we cannot be certain of the answer. For the criteria which we use necessarily arise from the sphere which we seek to examine. Nevertheless, our undertaking is not meaningless: we ask after our needs, and in a variety of different ways see how these can be thwarted or manipulated. We ask about our possibilities and become aware that we do not exhaust them – on the grounds of our own or others' failure. The great catchword through which we become conscious of all this is 'alienation'.

The various forms of human alienation, as a result of economic conditions, constraints or manipulation, cause infinitely great suffering. But their scope would be limited if as a result of insight and initiative the necessary changes could be introduced; if human alienation came from outside, and this alienation did not derive from man's self as such.

In that case man would need only to discover his identity and fight to realize it; the alienation would be external and not internal. In that case the power of alienation could be attributed to some demonic conditions or circumstances and not to man himself; he could defend himself against it like St George fighting the dragon. Once one actually confronts evil, it is possible to raise a lance, and the fight makes sense for a moment, even if in the end one succumbs. But what if man recognized his alienation precisely in the fact that he cannot exist at all without being exposed to alienating influences and even producing these himself? What if he were not only an alienated but also an alienating being? In that case he would live in a hopeless and absurd situation; the removal of his alienation would be conceivable only as a removal of man himself.

But the man who is unhappy with himself and makes others unhappy, the man who can only be freed from his alienated and alienating self by his death, will gain life – even before death and in a way which puts death in the shade! This is the discovery which struck Luther like a thunderbolt when he was studying Romans, and which constantly dawns afresh on men who feel alienated from themselves. I may be at odds with myself, I may not in the last resort feel able to live with myself, to be at peace with myself, much less with other people, but God wills to come close to me – cheering me, supporting me, liberating me and encouraging me. My present reality, alienated and alienating, does not have the last word; God wills to give us value, without our giving value to anything or to ourselves. The fact that God promises us our worth means the end of our own claims to worth and the beginning of a new confidence with ourselves and with one another. God wills to give us value, renounces his own value, and on the cross

39

of Jesus Christ exposes it to alienation, misunderstanding and mockery, to give value to us men.

From this Luther concludes that what we want to achieve by ourselves cannot prove successful, indeed that all our desires for human assertion must be laughable, unrealistic or rash. Here he can refer to Paul's anthropology and take up phrases from tradition (specifically from Augustine) which at the same time are made more radical: the 'desires' which fill men go beyond the sexual sphere; 'pride' is far more than a vice which makes a disagreeable impression on other people, and 'self-love' is not just an attitude which detracts from our love of our neighbours. All these, rather, are characteristics of the man who has a fixation on himself, is bent in on himself and incapable of walking upright; without God's intervention he has no choice but to be forced in on himself more and more, so that eventually he perishes. Here sin is understood as a reality which goes beyond morality and beyond our empirical world: we can see the consequences of it in our morality and our empirical experience all too clearly, but it cannot really be grasped, attacked or removed by our morality and our empirical potentialities.

Vicious circles

Luther goes on to speak in a vivid way of the devil, not just to relieve man of a burden but to demonstrate how men are caught up in their ungodliness in a way which transcends morality and our empirical experience, and to express its universal, indeed cosmic, scope. Sin, death and the devil form a power-complex which can only be broken by God's goodness, because man and the world are quite simply helpless in the face of it. Man is born into this situation: the term 'original sin', which so easily lends itself

40

to misunderstanding, is meant to indicate that there is no human life outside this interplay of sin, death and the devil, which awakens primal sin to new reality in every human life.

That sounds mediaeval, and does not please modern sensibilities. On the other hand, once again it is easier for us today to be aware of the transcendental interrelationships in which the individual lives and to which he has obligations. It is not just that we are more aware of the ambivalence of our involvement, our knowledge and our ability. Whatever we may invent, from the mallet to atomic power, from the alphabet to the computer, can become a blessing or a curse. Even worse are the vicious circles in which men are now entangled all over the world: poverty, hunger and terror, exploitation and being exploited, the political impotence of the individual and the impossibility of breaking out of an exploitative society, the increasing speed with which threatening developments progress, the general sense of aimlessness in our human existence. It is manifestly not enough for man to reflect on the basic circumstances of his existence and to remove one or two disruptive factors of which he becomes aware in reference to his relationship to his fellow-men, himself and his horizon of meaning: not only are the basic relationships of human existence destroyed; as far as we know them, they are themselves already indications of a fall. To adopt the terminology used by Tillich, there is no way in which man comes into existence which does not at the same time follow the lines of his fall; no way of being a man which does not at the same time involve being a sinner. To go back to the imagery I used previously, it is not a matter of the basic structures of humanity remaining intact, at least at foundation level, so that perhaps there is still a basement fit to live in. The building site must be excavated all over again, and if the old ruins are not removed, they will get in the way of the new building.

To abandon the imagery: any attempt at fulfilment which forgot these trans-moral and trans-empirical presuppositions, which in its quest for the 'self' sought realization in the sphere of 'action', would not just remain barren: because of the circumstances from which it began and the laws which it followed, it would succeed only in making things worse. What natural man regarded as fulfilment would in fact serve to destroy him. The climax of Luther's arguments is focussed on moral and religious fulfilment. Precisely in realizing his 'best potentialities' man succeeds in perfecting his self-deception, and the circle of the incurvation of his heart is inexorably completed.

Here the concept of sin may seem to be a negative one, but in fact it has a completely positive function. Sin is something that has to be overcome in the name of God. It cannot be overcome in the name of man. Talk of sin is not meant to disqualify man morally and finally to force in on him the hopelessness of his situation; it is meant to make clear to him that any fulfilment which is to be more than a psychologically satisfying combination of vitality, the capacity to impose oneself and the skilful use of possibilities needs another basis. This basis exists, is at our disposal and can be tested. If fulfilment is only a psychological or sociological programme, it always involves two dangers. If it seems to succeed within the limits imposed upon it, fulfilment can make people arrogant and élitist. If it does not succeed – and there is always something which will remain unfulfilled – it leads to a feeling of failure, of resignation, perhaps of despair. Christian theology tenaciously hangs on to talk of sin to make men aware that they must not be satisfied with the narrow-minded fulfilment of their own selves.

Christianity dares to assert that the empirical self is not identical with the real self. Whatever we experience in our day-to-day activities, whatever we gain from reflection or even from a professional analysis extending over a number of years, even what other people think of us and must think of us on the basis of the distinctive picture which we present – is not our real self.

By this assertion, Christianity creates room for movement in two respects: no one can be nailed down to a particular picture in which he appears, with or without his own guilt; no man can be measured adequately by his achievements or by the degree of his fulfilment understood in psychological or sociological terms. Max Frisch has urgently impressed on his readers that they are not to make 'an image' of others; that they must keep shattering the empirical image which appears, with an eye to a reality which transcends everything that can be fixed by imagery or empiricism. It is no coincidence that there is an analogy between this suggestion and that basic Old Testament commandment 'not to make an image or any other likeness'. There is nothing against relating this solemn 'prohibition of images' to our fellow men in the full sense of a divine commandment. The early Israelites and the pious rabbis have provided us with a model which we can apply today. A pictorial representation would not be able to express the reality standing behind it. What does that mean for our preoccupation with pictures as mementoes, with photograph albums and amateur films, with press photographs, and finally with the image of our fellow-men that we see before us with our own eyes, three feet away? Pious Jews never spoke the name of Yahweh – what does that mean for the way in which we deal with a name that we read beside a bell-push, that we hear on the telephone, indeed for the names that we give our children? When the rabbis spoke of God, they respectfully added, 'Blessed be he' – how would it be if after the names of our fellow-men we added a tacit 'all honour to him/her'? What applies to the picture that others make of us, or we make of them, also applies to the difference between our own real selves and our empirical selves. We should not trip ourselves up by constantly fixing ourselves in a picture that we have of ourselves. Naturally, a picture of ourselves has been suggested to us in the course of our lives: as Max Frisch would say, parents and grandparents, friends, colleagues and opponents, have 'had their share in creating it'; they have all read something into us, and our never-resting estimation of ourselves has added something else. But we need neither be proud of what has resulted from all this, nor need we despair over it. To put it in an exaggerated way, we might say: don't worry – your real self is something different from what you think you can recognize it to be!

It is certainly important to establish once and for all this difference between empirical and real self, even without filling in the content. The empirical self gains something from it: it can breathe again. However, this distinction can only be substantiated and justified when I can define the 'real self' in more detail. Otherwise the suspicion would arise that this was a piece of evasive action by the empirical self under pressure, no longer able to cope with the factors that make it up.

I, yet not I

Christianity affirms that it is possible to distinguish between the real self and the empirical self, not on the basis of theoretical considerations, but on the basis of an empirical datum – if a historical fact can be described in that way. The historical fact is that a certain Jesus of Nazareth was born, lived, suffered, was crucified and died among men. No one can do away with this fact. Whether people know about it or not, whether they interpret it like Christians (who of course disagree very much about it among themselves) or otherwise; whether they deny it or ignore it – nothing can alter the fact that we have faces like this Jesus, that Jesus too belongs to mankind. Anyone who has been born since then lives as a man 'after the birth of Christ', and all those who lived before, lived in a humanity in which Christ was to be born. Karl Barth puts it like this: 'The ontological determination of humanity is grounded in the fact that one man among all others is the man Jesus. . . We cannot break free from this neighbour. He is definitively our neighbour. And we as men are those among whom Jesus is also a man, like us for all his unlikeness. . . In him we have the central human factor.'[26] That this fact of Jesus as our neighbour is more important for men than our affinity to those many other people who make up the history of mankind, and without whom that history would not be as we see it today, has not been discovered by professional anthropologists, nor is it established on the basis of general agreement, nor has it been decreed by a dominant group. It is the experience of men who had doubt in themselves or who were shaken in their self-confidence; the experience of men who had only modest possibilities and success in terms of any fulfilment that could be achieved by psychology or sociology. We are told of unstable psychological cases or sick people, of the lame, of women who had only a very lowly status in their world, of a once stubborn fisherman called Peter, of a Jewish theologian by the name of Paul who was at first very sure of himself and his cause. By taking their new neighbour

45

Jesus seriously, these people had an overwhelming experience. Their former self-awareness was overthrown; they could leave behind their previous experiences, with themselves and others, and begin their life again. Some spoke of 'rebirth'; they felt free and as though new-born; once again they were right at the beginning, which this time did not lead to a sorry, all too familiar end. Others spoke of a 'new creation': the old had passed; incredibly, but finally, in an empirically tangible form, the new had begun. This new creation was so alien to them that they could not recognize it any longer as something of their own. 'I live,' one of them said, 'yet not I'; this new neighbour fills me completely and lives in me (Gal. 2.20).

Christian theology attempted to understand the experiences of men with this man Jesus, who burst the familiar framework of human existence, with the help of the thought-forms at its disposal. If talk of God was to have any sense, it had to be related to this new neighbour Jesus and had to be illuminated by him. The birth of man's new self was grounded in the birth of Jesus, and in his life and death (which for him could not have the last word). 'See,' Luther preached with enthusiasm, 'in this way Christ takes our birth from us and sinks it in his birth, and give us his, so that we become pure and new in it, as though it were our own.' Or in another context, 'God who created me is my cousin, closest friend; is my flesh and blood. If nothing but that – enough!'[27]

Understood in this way, man's real self is not something that man can realize by himself, something he can only muddle along with. It is a gift, the trans-empirical basis to which the empirical self can constantly relate, the trans-moral presupposition from which all our morality continually derives its force and its power. There is another indication that it is a gift and not something that man can

46

make for himself; not an attitude in which man can train himself; not an oasis of psychological rest to which we can gain access at any time by our own concentration. The empirical self often perceives and becomes sure of the real self in the most unexpected ways. It seems apart from our control and yet capable of being experienced, as when one of us speaks to another of our neighbour Jesus, when the so-called gospel begins to kindle a light in its hearers, a light which consists in the knowledge that we will not come to grief because our make-up has been moulded by our empirical self and thus by sin. The success of our life is not in question, but is already fulfilled, already assured, in advance of ourselves and the horizon of our experiences at the time. We may accept ourselves within the problematical structures of our empirical selves; we do not have to 'realize' ourselves, create our own reality and increase it, heighten it and intensify it; we do not have to protect ourselves against nothingness. Quite apart from ourselves we can be sure of an indestructible make-up, ground of being and fulfilment. In that case the realization of our humanity will no longer be an aim which we pursue with every means at our disposal, energetically and with perseverance, so that we get at least half way there. In that case, rather, knowledge of our real self will provide a base from which we can depart with complete security in order to discover the consequences of the specific form of our fulfilment.

In that case, too, while the question how far I am to pursue or renounce my empirical fulfilment is by no means unimportant, it is certainly secondary. For whatever happens, 'Whatever we do, in word or deed, we do in the name of the Lord Jesus, giving thanks to God the Father through him' (Col. 3.17).

5   *God – The Embodiment of Fulfilment*

God said to Moses 'I will be who I will be,'
and said, 'Say this to the people of Israel,
"I will be" has sent me to you.'

Exodus 3.14

Karl Rahner once said, 'Thank God that what sixty to eighty per cent of people conceive of as God does not exist.'[28] His remark might seem almost cynical. Christian theologians must bear a good deal of blame for the fact that 'sixty to eighty per cent of people' drag round with them a conception of God which tends more to hinder them from understanding the concern of the gospel and the meaningfulness of their humanity which it expresses. Sunday-school teachers and teachers of religion are equally at fault. I write as one who also bears the blame.

How did it come about that God is not regarded more as a counter-symbol to human fulfilment than as its embodiment, its ground and its perspective – among both believers and unbelievers? That he appears as a zealous and vindictive phantom monster from the science-fiction world of primaeval times, to whom the men of those days in some incomprehensible way sacrificed possessions and strength, understanding and freedom, indeed even themselves and one another?

The history of Christian theology contains an abundance of new attempts to show that the God of Jesus Christ is 'other', that whatever men understand by God cannot be

48

God for that very reason. 'Whatever a finite being understands is finite,' was Thomas Aquinas' verdict.[29] 'God can only be God by being, thinking and knowing in a different way from ourselves,' says Luther.[30] But Christian theology has not carried through the 'prohibition against images' in a sufficiently radical way, has not taken seriously enough the fact that from its perspective there could only be one legitimate reason for breaking the prohibition of images and saying of God more than that we can say nothing about him. That reason is Jesus Christ.

Supreme being

A theology which wanted to know who or what God 'is' would have to relate him to what we understand by 'being' elsewhere: his 'reality' would have to be explained in its relationship to our reality. This prompts two patterns of thinking. On the one hand one could think of God's reality as authentic reality, as 'supreme being', in the face of which every entity that we perceive on earth has only a derived existence and thus in the last resort remains inauthentic and, measured by God's reality, unreal. In other words, entities only take on their own reality through their relationship to God. That is the course which has been taken by Western scholasticism – embracing in a complicated way Plato and Aristotle – and its more or less orthodox new versions. On the other hand, the alternative model has not found so much recognition within the framework of Christian theology. Here the earthly experience of the existence of the entity formed the starting point. It was then argued that to ascribe such existence to God would be quite inadequate; by that standard God is more than being, indeed he is 'free from being', he is 'nothing'. This is the line taken by mysticism, which could of course establish many links with scholastic themes. God's being is such, argues Nicholas of Cusa, 'that he neither is nor is not, nor is and at the same time is not, nor is or at the same time is not'[31] – all these statements do not 'touch' God. In that case human fulfilment – in this context the very term is misleading – would consist in forgetting entities and the self: 'If the soul is to see God, it may not see anything in time; for so long as the soul is aware of time or space or any conception of this kind, it can never know God. If the soul is to know God, it must also forget itself and must lose itself; for as long as it sees and knows itself, it does not see and know God. . . .'[32] Such forgetfulness of self also sets it free for complete abandonment to doing the good. Detaching themselves from Neo-Platonic presuppositions, the Reformers later took over some of them.

Protestant orthodoxy by no means despised scholasticism. On this basis it was possible to gain all kinds of further information about the being and reality of God. God was free, at one with himself, happy in himself; he was self-sufficient and at the same time was the foundation of all things; he bestowed reality and then took it away again. God was endowed with a complicated system of attributes which were assigned him on the basis of biblical statements or philosophical considerations, and which were inferred from human experience. In the eyes of those with less of a philosophical education, or those who were no longer able to share the traditional philosophical presuppositions, God threatened to become an other-wordly super-being with human characteristics extended to the ultimate degree. His reality and human reality began to compete with each other. God's reality seemed unattainable and its connection with earthly reality was barely recognizable. Did God's reality leave the reality of the world in the lurch, or did it even threaten the reality of the world?

50

Did talk of the existence of God rob man of his dignity? Did the reality of God exclude the fulfilment of a mature man, who could shape his life and his society by exercising his own control? The concept of God arrived at an impasse: some said that it simply reflected man's longing for grandeur, freedom and fulfilment, while others felt that if the concept of God did not really help man towards more grandeur, freedom and fulfilment, it was high time for him to be rid of it. Talk of the reality of God seemed to be a useless instrument, indeed a dangerous obstacle, as far as human fulfilment was concerned. But, as Feuerbach rightly pointed out, this was the God whom man had made in his own image – as a result of his insatiable hunger for more of his own reality. Some theologians in our century then discovered that this God was dead – in other words, the men had died who could see their reality assured and increased by the projection of such a conception of God. New patterns took over this function. People no longer saw any need to cannibalize or manipulate Christian traditions; the pictures of God which men had painted so zealously began to fade and no one restored their colours. And now, as a result, it is possible once again to talk of the God of Jesus Christ in the imagelessness of his origin.

I am who I am

When Moses in the wilderness was given the task of announcing his resistance to Pharaoh and liberating the people of Israel from their situation of slavery, he was not clear what authentication he was to give. It was not enough for him to appeal to the God of the patriarchs. The God who sent him could not be defined solely in terms of the previous experiences which men had had of him. He sought to reveal himself – so the biblical tradition affirms – as the

51

one who said of himself: 'I will be who I will be' (Ex. 3.14). It did not occur to the Israelites to misunderstand this unique name as a philosophical definition of the reality of God. It announced to them one who at the same time would remain a complete mystery to them – not to be pinned down and thus not at God's disposal, always new, surprising, always in advance, not to be classified and yet identical with himself, true to himself. 'I will be who I will be' is formally a tautology: the stone is a stone, the tree is a tree, God is God, saying nothing and precisely in so doing keeping the inexpressible secret: I am I. Here no further questioning is possible, there can be no additional argument: a 'logical stop signal' (van Buren/Ramsey). 'I will be who I will be' – that is the name of God which may not be misused, which must be hallowed, a name which goes beyond the bounds of a name and yet in so doing makes clear something of the nature of every name. 'I' am not only this or that, the one who is named in this way or another, the one who is to be described through this or that. Above all, first and foremost, I am 'I'.

The Israelites also read something else out of this self-designation of their God. They did not have any theoretical, abstract concept of being like the Greeks. They did not use the word 'is' at all in everyday language; it had to be supplied in accordance with the sense of the statement. When there was express mention of 'being', as in the name of their God, this was being in relationship, being in its significance for something else. Therefore the 'I will be' in this name is to be understood as the promise, 'I will be there, present, effective, for you.' Although you Israelites will have some surprises about me, although I will keep breaking through your attempts to grasp me by your expectations and conceptions, there is one thing on which you can rely, one thing in which you can grasp me; I will be there for you. The reality of Yahweh consists in his being there for his people; the reality of God consists in his being there for men. All further questioning as to whether and in what way the reality of God must first 'be there', before it can be there and effective for others, comes up against the mystery of God's underivative promise of himself. The God of Israel does not reveal himself as the one who *is*, who is permanent, superior to all that is transitory and pressing in upon it, but as the one who is faithful *par excellence*, as the one who remains true to himself by being true to all those who encounter him, as the one who promises to every man a tacit, absolutely reliable 'I am there', which can be claimed at any time.

The Israelites were able also to understand God as the God of 'their fathers', to understand him as the Lord 'their' God through his actions and words, in the same way as we can sometimes recognize from the fact that a person says to us 'I am the one who . . .' that we have already encountered each other before somewhere.

One last thing is striking about the Old Testament name for God: the tense in which it is expressed. ' "I will be there" has sent me to you.' That is what Moses is to say to the astounded Israelites. This, too, is connected with the Hebrew use of language; they do not talk of purely present existence – e.g. the moment which is so beautiful in itself. For them, all time, and everything of which time can be predicated, belongs either to the past or to the time that is not yet past, namely, the future. God is eternal in being eternally future. Ernst Bloch has coined the phrase that here we find God 'with the future as his mode of being'. It is the future of his fidelity which marks out the God of Israel. He realizes himself in the future of his concern as the one who 'is and was and is to be' (Rev. 1.4).

What do these far-fetched ideas mean for our fulfilment,

for the fulfilment of the believer? First, that in the Old Testament name for God we are presented with a model of 'fulfilment' about which we are ambivalent. Man may understand himself as a mystery, but he can see quite clearly a number of factors which govern his existence. His assertion 'I am I' contains a considerable amount of stubbornness, defensiveness and aggression. 'We are ourselves and write that down' goes a South German phrase which illustrates this quite clearly. While a man may understand his life to some degree as being there for others, it cannot be disputed that his life is also inconceivable without the existence of others. Life – and this also applies to its non-human forms – is giving and taking, voluntarily and as a matter of course, or as a result of compulsion and force: it is never exclusively spontaneous for others. While our self may be reflected in the experiences which others have or have had of us, it is not a good thing for people to measure us by what they have come to know of us. Indeed, we are grateful when they do not. The difference between the model of fulfilment provided by the Old Testament name for God and our own reality is clearest in its last characteristic, namely its utter futurity: empirical observation suggests to us that I will not be the one who I will be, but I am the one who will not be.

Thus the Old Testament name for God is only of very limited use as a model for human fulfilment. Perhaps it is worthwhile for men to strive for futurity as such, but hardly for the futurity of a mysterious, unconditional being-there for others. What we see here is not only impossible as a guideline for our human fulfilment; it would be an illusory, arrogant and catastrophic misunderstanding of our reality. We cannot and should not be what the Old Testament says of its God and holds him out to be, either for ourselves, for others or for the non-human creation.

54

The identity of Jesus

When the people who met Jesus asked themselves what there was about him, 'God' and 'Son of God' were the highest titles of honour that they could bestow. In fact, it was really impermissible to call a man by such titles, since that amounted to blasphemy. However, those who experienced Jesus' concern, and began to join him on his way, understood that here was a man who burst the bounds of what had previously been seen as human fulfilment, a man who could not be explained completely in terms of human origins, whose sacrifice for his fellow men in the last resort knew no limits, to whom the future belonged as it did to no other man. Here we are confronted with the hope associated with the name of God, with his name 'I will be who I will be', in human form and in a specific situation, there for us and remaining there for us in a mysterious way which cannot be established, taking our being and abiding character upon himself, guaranteeing and disclosing to us the hope bound up with the name of God, 'I will be who I will be'. The figure of Jesus of Nazareth, his life, suffering and dying, appeared as a fulfilment of the God whose name showed him to be underived and unfathomable, irresistibly and unconditionally there for men. Of course this was surprising and unexpected, but in the last resort it was at least consistent. The Old Testament name for God helped to understand the reality of Jesus; the models for human identity previously in use proved to be inadequate.

Those who met Jesus and talked about him felt that he was the man he wanted to be. Nothing that arose from the depths of his own existence nor any external circumstances could prevent him from being the one who he was, who he 'had to' be, as the gospels occasionally put it. To this degree he can be described as 'the most fortunate man who ever lived'.[33] But his good fortune did not come without a struggle, nor his identity without a crisis: the story of his threefold temptation in the wilderness may preserve a memory of this. He could have been other than he was; he could have claimed and presented the possibility of his otherness. The story of the temptation expressed this possibility in symbols: bread for his own existence; immunity from danger for his own person; power and recognition for his legitimate claim to the kingdom of the world. But Jesus recalled that he lived from the word that came through the mouth of God; that it was his food to do the will of God; that he had been 'sent' and had 'come' to give his life for many. One of the earliest hymns to be composed and sung about him affirms this precisely. He 'did not count it robbery to be equal with God' (Phil. 2.6), he did not care about it, the claim meant nothing to him, he did not exploit the opportunity as would have been quite legitimate for him. 'He was God,' Luther explained, 'and all the divine words and works that he does he did for our benefit and thus serves us as a slave . . . he did not seek either honour or goodness there, but our good and our salvation . . .'[34] He 'emptied himself', 'took the form of a slave', 'humbled himself', 'was obedient to death, even death on the cross'. However, all this did not result in the loss of his identity and the collapse of his selfhood. In all this a life was fulfilled; in all this – as we would say, using more modern terminology – he realized himself. He knew not only the temptation to exploit his own potentialities but also the oppressiveness of human existence, forced into a corner by the threat of torture and death, the experience of 'the soul being troubled, even to death'. He did not withstand this heroically, but in a childlike prayer whispered 'Abba, my Father!' And according to a comment in the Gospel of Luke, an angel had to come to him and strengthen him:

56

artists from the baroque period have portrayed a powerful angel supporting him and holding him up. With the cry, 'My God, why have you forsaken me?', he gives up his identity, gives it into the hands of the Father. The cry of desperation is the verse of a psalm, part of a prayer: in surrendering his identity he found this identity fulfilled. He is the grain of wheat which only brings forth fruit if it dies. In this way the divine name 'I will be for you who I will be for you' is again made specific in an unexpected way. By breaking bread and drinking wine at his last supper with the disciples, Jesus says, 'This is what I am, you can live from this; this is my body and blood, my existence, my identity, given for you so that your existence, your identity, your ego does not perish in the face of everything that puts it in question.'

Jesus achieves his identity by coming to terms with his origin and his destiny, by coming to terms with the 'Father' and the 'brethren', who immediately recognize him as the bread of life and the light of the world, as the way on which they can go and the door which has been opened for them. In what he says, the thing that impresses them is the deliberate 'But I . . .' with which he sets himself – and them – above traditions which have hitherto been respected. All that he does is illuminated by his indescribable 'I am', which fulfils all their longing and at the same time kindles it afresh, which puts living and dying in a new light. Luther interprets it in this way: 'the glory of our God', his consummation, the way in which he is God, is that, 'for our sakes he gives himself utterly, in the flesh, in the bread, in our mouth, heart and breast. . .'[35] God fulfils himself in the sending of his Son, in the coming of his kingdom, and the fulfilment of the believer has its place and its guarantee in God's own fulfilment of himself. God's fulfilment of himself is in no way excluded here. It lies in the future, is still to come, just as it has always been unexpected: the first Christians expressed this in a way which seemed obvious to them by talking of their expectation of the return of Christ and the dawn of the kingdom of God: 'Amen, yes, come Lord Jesus!' (Rev. 22.20).

The Spirit

In the liturgical language of the church, the old gesture of longing is that of holding up arms outstretched to heaven. This is the way in which the priest in traditional rites, or any believer who belongs to a charismatic movement, prays for the descent of the Holy Spirit. By his external attitude, the person praying indicates that he has nothing to offer and that he is wholly intent on receiving. He is open, prepared to receive the gift which comes to him from above, full of longing for 'the burden of the spirit', as the late-mediaeval mystic Christina Ebnerin put it. One ancient symbol for the evasiveness of the divine is the wind which no one can grasp: it blows where it wills, intensifies to become a storm and then dies down again to a hardly detectable breeze. Another is the flight of the birds who fly in unpredictable circles through the sky, form a flock and break apart again, or suddenly descend upon a tree: for a while they fly in and out among the branches, settle for a moment, and then unexpectedly fly off again.

This imagery expresses a contradictory and painful experience. In our search for the fulfilment of our life we want to lay ourselves open – and yet we cannot grasp and hold what we long for. We are drawn to a reality outside our own reality, to a reality for which we cannot find the appropriate terms in our own vocabulary yet which nevertheless already works in us as an unquenchable desire. The Spirit to which we want to open ourselves has long been present and carefully at work in the movement of our arms as they open, in the movement of our heart as it softens and turns to longing.

I remember very vividly how at the end of one session of a seminar a student, who was to read a paper about the Holy Spirit at the next session, ceremoniously opened a packet which he had brought with him and produced the carved wooden figure of a Buddha dancing in ectasy. As preparation for his lecture he wanted his fellow students to ask themselves whether this Buddha had the Holy Spirit. The longing for fulfilment lives in all men, and all religions give expression to it. Similarly, in the secular world we hear talk of the 'spirit' of a revolution, of a treaty, of a particular day, which bears witness to such a longing. To have this spirit, to be filled with it and allow oneself to be driven by it, would then be authentic, meaningful life; it would be fulfilment which no longer allows itself to be bounded by the superficial, temporal limitations of the self.

Christianity, too, knows of the unique relationship between the longings of the human heart, indeed of creation apart from man, and the divine spirit. However, at this point it is remarkably reserved. It prohibits man from finding rest in the ecstasy of the dance, from being himself in contemplation or in action. The hands of the pious may not close round the mystery. Faith is concerned that the arms of longing remain open, that people do not allow themselves to be satisfied too readily or to be content with substitute offers. Faith radicalizes the expectation of human fulfilment; the level of demand rises. The Holy Spirit, as Christianity understands it, does not promise man an end to the opposition between frustration and desire, but the capacity to tolerate tensions between longing and fulfilment and to make creative use of them. As a Christian, I will be less satisfied with the realities of my life at any one time

59

than my friend who understands himself from the perspective of, say, humanist psychology. On the other hand, as a Christian I begin from the fact that God himself is in process of fulfilling himself, unfolding his mysterious being for others, expressing it and bringing it to consummation. Thus it is inappropriate for me to allow myself to be troubled by aspects of my personal reality at a particular time, to become impatient and embark on over-hasty initiatives. Rather, one thing in particular is important for me: to become involved in the process of God's fulfilment, to find my place in it, to allow myself to be taken up into its mysterious trends and movements – and this is what, according to Christian conceptions, the Spirit of God seeks to 'achieve' in a man by bringing him to belief in Jesus Christ.

Christianity does not understand the self-realization of God as an overpowering process to which man need only surrender; it is a directed undertaking, a 'covenant', as the Bible says. Its content was not disclosed to the first Christians in general religious principles: for them the all-important thing was encounter with the man Jesus of Nazareth, his vision of the kingdom of God, his dedication, the way in which he dealt with the bungled past and present of those with whom he spoke, the way he ate with them and died for them. He himself proved decisive for any future talk about 'God': he showed why there were men at all, why there was a 'creation'; and he himself was responsible for men understanding this fact and beginning to accept that he was the one person relevant for them and for the whole of life. This caused offence in a way which believers and non-believers alike can sense even today. In the gospels it is said that 'flesh and blood' cannot escape it, and in Luther's Little Catechism it is simply accepted with the words: 'I believe that I can believe in Jesus Christ, my

Lord, or come to him, not by virtue of my own reason or strength.' The community attributes to the 'Spirit' the fact that Jesus can nevertheless be acknowledged as the Christ, that he is the source of consolation and the power to change: 'No one can say "Jesus is Lord" except by the Holy Spirit' (I Cor. 12.3). It is the Holy Spirit which puts suggestions to men and makes it possible for them to relate the relevance of Jesus to the whole course of the world; to seek and to make use of their own place in this process; to look for the radical and universal power of this saving relevance and to live for it. We read in the Bible, 'The Spirit himself bears witness with our spirit that we are children of God' (Rom. 8.16). The Spirit enables us to recognize, perceive and take our place in the process of the self-realization of God.

Eastern theology and spirituality has never forgotten that the believer not only stands over against God but also has his being 'in God' and 'God in him'. Hence Serapion of Thmuis (died AD 362), a bishop and theologian of the early church, could pray with his congregation to God for the identity of the believers, for adequate fulfilment and for a true and full life:

> We pray thee, make us living men; give us the Spirit of Light, that we may know the True One and him whom thou hast sent, Jesus Christ. Give us the Holy Spirit, that we may be able to utter and explain thy inexpressible mysteries. May the Lord Jesus Christ speak in us, and the Holy Spirit praise Thee through us.[36]

Trinity as a model – a proposal

The prayer of Serapion opens up contexts of human fulfilment which hardly seem attainable to the modern reader, yet which nevertheless can perhaps exercise a certain fascination on him: to be a living man evidently means to know God in the 'Spirit of Light' – him, the 'true', the one who is authentic, reliable, faithful *par excellence*, to whose nature it belongs that he has entered into a relationship with us, that he has sent us a message, indeed a messenger, Jesus Christ. The mysterious connection between this messenger and his origin, an inexpressible mystery, can be expressed and explained (certainly not in a modern intellectual-type sense) only if the very one of whom we are to speak utters the word in us, if the one who calls us at the same time answers in us and from us. Thus while the believer is on the one hand confronted with God as the 'wholly other', on the other hand he is as it were drawn into the mystery of the triune God, into the dynamic of fulfilment. That may sound presumptuous to modern ears, or even abstract and remote from the world. The doctrine of the Trinity plays no part in the life of the churchgoer without any interest in theology; on the contrary, for him it is a diffuse and unnecessary calculation without value for present-day belief and action. Those who have steeped themselves in the history of the origin and interpretation of this dogma may have been made even more sceptical. However, we need not go into detail here. I find what Serapion says in his prayer to be important and illuminating for the following reasons. The last decade of theological discussion has been marked by the question how we can talk of God and whether he exists at all; whether here we do not have a product of human imagination and wishful thinking. The God whom philosophers regard as impossible, and whose death is asserted even by Christian theologians, was certainly not the God of Serapion of Thmuis. Rather, he was a God who had been imagined as a kind of super-being, endowed with human traits and capacities, only not subject to human limitations. A hymn from the nineteenth century describes him as 'the one who sits enthroned on the stars for ever and ever'. However, he manifestly did not sit enthroned on the stars and did not govern the world. What did he do? Where could his rule be found in Auschwitz? If he existed at all, in the last resort did he not pose a threat to man coming of age? This God was intolerable for men – he had to be killed, if he had not been dead long since.

There is a quite remarkable fact which is of particular importance for our question of fulfilment. The man who no longer wanted to be threatened by the theistic God had understood himself in terms of the model of the God he wanted to remove. He himself wanted to govern and shape the world in his own way, with full power, in supreme perfection and the utmost efficiency. He understood himself in the shadow of a picture of God which provided for power and freedom at the expense of other subordinate powers or people. This gave rise to a vision of fulfilment which consisted in the exploitation of every possibility, in the use of every chance to one's own advantage, in the devouring of sacrifices – Brother Roger's vision of the leech! No wonder that this programme for fulfilment not only turned man against man, but in the last resort pulled down into the abyss the God who had served as a model for it.

Had the knowledge of the triune God who involves men in his own fulfilment remained alive in Christianity, presumably a death-of-God theology could never have arisen. In that case, at any rate, it would have been clear that God may not be misunderstood as something that 'is' (or 'cannot be'): neither theism nor atheism provide an appropriate philosophical perspective for the triune God. In that case it would have had to be remembered that God cannot be brought under a particular heading, whether of 'process', 'co-humanity' or anything else. The very term 'God' must lead to misunderstandings if one does not begin in the same breath to tell of Jesus Christ and God's Spirit, of creation, redemption and consummation. One cannot talk 'simply' of God because he is 'trinity'.

This also has interesting consequences for the problem of human fulfilment. The man who is created in the 'image of God' cannot then be the autonomous, self-centred egoist, using his natural powers to the last extremity. What a mystery it is (no easier to understand than the divine Trinity) that each of us already finds that we are involved in the tension of being woman or man, being in relationship, subordinate to a 'you', produced from a 'we' and born into a 'we'! The fact that a human being is always involved in a relationship of I, you and we is no construction imposed at a later stage, no consequence of humanity. Rather, it is a basic condition of our origin and our reality, which already presages the only form which fulfilment can take.

Life in the first person, directed towards others and in the light of others, in a community that can be referred to as 'we', means to practise concern, to experience concern, to stand in the power and the communion of mutual concern. The church father Augustine thought that he could perceive in God himself this threefold element, which he saw as a 'trace of the Trinity' in man. He therefore defined God as the lover, the beloved and the love which exists between the two.

There are questions that I might ask without meaning to attack the mystery of the Trinity or to resolve or profane it. Do I not need the Father, the ground of my being, who accepts me and in whom I am assured of my ultimate support? Do I not also need the Son and brother who makes possible and justifies my being in relationship to the

64

Father? Do I not also need the good Spirit who assures me of my nearness to Father and Son and allows me to live in his strength? I might put it in yet another way. To whom may I be father, to whom may I give assurances about the ground of his being by listening to him, putting my hand on his shoulder and comforting him? To whom may I be son, pleading his cause, fighting for his concerns and realizing his future? Finally, to whom may I be the inspiring spirit, father and son alike, by prompting visions in him and encouraging him along the way to freedom?

We may have many psychological, sociological and even theological hesitations about talking of Father, Son and Spirit in this way. I would brush them aside and ask: could not the Christian tradition help to disclose what it means to be father, to be mother, to be daughter, to be son, to be life-giving spirit? All this seems remote from the classic doctrine of the Trinity. But it does suggest to me the utopia of a humanity in which people relate to one another as fathers and sons, mothers and daughters, sisters and brothers, in the power of mutual devotion and love.

Life between God and God

For years I have been haunted by a phrase from notes of a conversation by a sick-bed. The pastoral counsellor, still inexperienced but full of good will, had said something about God's goodness to a terminally ill patient. After a pause she replied, apparently directly, 'And the doctors are also so good to me . . .' Evidently to begin with she could make nothing of the idea of the goodness of God as it had been expressed by the counsellor. But the way in which the doctors cared for her gave her some inkling of what that could be – goodness which was related to her: God's goodness.

I would interpret this little incident in the following way. For the suffering patient the hands of the doctors represented God's concern, that of the Father; in the words of the counsellor she addressed as it were God the Son; and in the budding confidence in the goodness of God and man that surrounded her, God the Holy Spirit came into view. The believer understands his life as an event between God and God; in it he recognizes a collaboration of God with himself. He becomes aware of the inter-relationship of what may seem disparate to our awareness and our experience: on the one hand natural processes of life and historical developments, and on the other the claim of the relevance of Jesus Christ; on the one hand obvious traits of life which end in death and on the other the offer of a new life which in the end should break open the limitations of creaturely existence; on the one hand the results of scientific investigations and on the other the self-examination of a faith which appeals to the unfinished character of a specific historical event. In the language of earlier dogmatics: on the one hand the world of the Father, the Creator; on the other the world of the Son, the Redeemer, but in both instances the one God, perceived and praised through the one Spirit in the believing man who can relate the relevance of Jesus Christ to this whole reality which he experiences. Where Jesus becomes relevant as the Christ, human and ultimately non-human reality achieves fulfilment – and here God fulfils himself. The believer will not be surprised that humanistic concerns, psychology and sociology, achieve fulfilment in a way which seems very reminiscent of that of faith, and indeed sometimes appear to be identical with faith. Yet this must be the case if man's actual reality is to find its fulfilment in the relevance of Jesus Christ; if the Father is to have anything to do with the Son. The God who seeks to still human longing for a fulfilled life, to remove the opposition which arises against it, and indeed to redeem the sighing and anxious creation is the God who fulfils himself in the creation of the world and of man. The believer gratefully perceives this and invites the non-believer to share his perception that human hope and love and the specific figure and message of Jesus complement each other.

While writing these last pages I have had in mind some imagery which one can often find in the Catholic churches of South Germany. Crowning the baroque altar-piece, surrounded by clouds and angels as a simple symbol for the heavenly world, there is a representation of the Holy Trinity: God the Father, with a crown and a flowing beard, and God the Son, with the marks of his wounds still visible, are sitting facing one another, and half way up is the Holy Spirit in the form of a dove. But between them, the three divine persons have a golden ball which is meant to symbolize the earth or the universe. The universe turns between God, Father, Son and Spirit: all life in it is lived out between God and God.

We cannot imitate the simplicity of the baroque artists, but I think that I understand what they are trying to say. I may understand my fulfilment in faith as a partial element of God's fulfilment; it is part of the ultimate destiny of all men and the whole world. It is part of a movement which does not come to a standstill at the limits of my own reality and the reality of the world which surrounds it: of a movement of love and being loved which goes beyond the limitations of our earthly love, caught up as it is in guilt. Even death will not be able to put a stop to it. I find myself taken up into a movement of love which will not tolerate my turning away; into a stream which carries me along -- into the shearing force of the fulfilment of the triune

God who in a mysterious way will be there for me in and beyond all the future.

6 *Fulfilment in Faith*

> Shortly before his death, Rabbi Sussya said: 'In the world to come they will not ask me, "Why were you not Moses?" They will ask me, "Why were you not Sussya?" '
>
> *Martin Buber*

Called to fulfilment

The believer feels that his empirical and moral reality is grounded and set in train outside himself. The significance of this trans-empirical and trans-moral grounding for any particular empirical self was disclosed to the men of the Bible when they were called. Moses, who in the wilderness is given the commission to free his people from slavery, does not just ask the name of the one who sends him. He also asks, 'Who am I, that I should go to Pharaoh and lead the children of Israel out of Egypt?' (Ex. 3.11). Of course this remark reveals anxiety and defensiveness, lack of self-confidence, knowledge that 'I' cannot really do what is expected of me. As the narrator of this story understands it, God accepts the fearfulness of his partner and assures him of his presence and support. The answer given to the question 'Who am I?' is 'I will be with you' (Ex. 3.12). Who am I? I am the one whom God wants with him! God shows himself as the one who in a mysterious way, quite beyond my control, will be there for me long beyond any conceivable future – here I recognize myself as the one to whom this divine promise is addressed, for whom it is

69

valid. I live by it; my self is grounded in it and has its fulfilment in it.

The people of the Bible did not respond to the call of God with a 'Yes', or a questioning, 'What's the matter?' Their response to the voice of God which they heard was, 'Lord, here I am' (Ex. 3.5; Gen. 22.1; I Sam. 3; Acts 9.10). As this 'Here I am' took effect in their lives, it became clear to them what they were saying when they used the word 'I'. This 'I' learnt to express its anxiety, its gratitude and its hope in the language of the psalms:

> When my soul was embittered, when I was pricked in heart, I was stupid and ignorant, I was like a beast towards thee. Nevertheless I am continually with thee; thou dost hold my right hand. Thou dost guide me with thy counsel, and afterward thou wilt receive me to glory. . .' (Ps. 73.22f.)

> I will extol thee, O Lord, for thou hast drawn me up, and hast not let my foes rejoice over me. O Lord my God, I cried to thee for help, and thou hast healed me. O Lord, thou hast brought up my soul from death. . . (Ps. 30.2ff.).

But the people of the Bible were also aware of the 'I' which resisted God: 'Lord, depart from me, for I am a sinful man' (Luke 5.8); the 'I' of the sinner who must have an ill opinion of himself and in terror asked Jesus at his last supper, 'Lord, is it I?' The 'I' of prophets and apostles took shape in a struggle with a divine calling; their biographies were written between 'resistance and surrender'. Jonah flees and has the most astonishing experiences in his flight before God; Jeremiah curses his mother for having given birth to him, and yet is filled with confidence: 'Thy words became to me a joy and the delight of my heart; for

70

I am called by thy name, O Lord, God of hosts'
(Jer. 15.10ff.).

In some circumstances the person called had to be told
explicitly who he had now become as a result of his call,
the direction in which his person had to be realized. 'You
are Peter; you need not continue to drag around your old
self and your former names. I am refashioning you, and
will build upon you as on a rock.' Something of this knowledge lives on in the custom of giving the Christian his
name at baptism. Before that, he or she is the son or
daughter of these parents or those, a fact which seems to
foreshadow the empirical self; baptism in the name of the
Trinity removes the limitations from this narrow programme of bourgeois fulfilment and takes it up into the
movement of God's realization of himself. No wonder that
the people of the Bible derived a considerable amount of
self-knowledge from their call: in it they discovered their
identity, so that they could say, with a self-confidence
which almost puts us moderns off from the start: 'I, Paul
. . . by the grace of God I am what I am' (cf. Gal. 5.2; I
Cor. 15.10). We should occasionally ask how far our modern concern for self-discovery, which is expressed in psychology or sociology, or our tacit presupposition that the
human self must have a specific fulfilment and realization,
could have been articulated without the biblical sense of
vocation. The believer knows that he has been called, and
his personal satisfaction must be the result rather than the
measure of his call. If I still attach importance to the
vocation to which I have been called, or think it important
that the position to which I am called should find general
acknowledgment and respect, then I have yet to understand God's call. Nevertheless, at the same time, it is also
not enough to remember Luther's now famous saying that
the girl who sweeps the yard or spreads manure is fulfilling

the true divine service which has been laid upon her. This may be her task for the moment, but she must also ask herself whether it is the way she is going to spend her whole life, whether there are criteria by which her action might no longer seem meaningful and in accord with her calling. When someone is called to fulfil himself in the train of God's own fulfilment, he acquires keen ears and sharp eyes for possibilities in the situation of the empirical self or its social environment which could be utilized or have to be rejected. Vocation makes the empirical self flexible and dynamic. Fulfilment in faith is achieved in the interplay between the call of God and the particular psychological, physical or social reality in which it takes place. The person called finds fulfilment to the degree to which he exposes his own psyche and nature, his biographical and social moulding, to the call which comes to him, and indeed puts himself in a position to hear that call in the first place. In that case his self is no longer limited to a programme provided by his heredity and environment; by responding to the call he gains the possibility of realizing more as it were than himself. The call provokes him to transcend his existing self, and his self takes shape in the interplay between its present reality and the call. Karl Barth concludes from this: 'Grow into your character, accept the outline of your particular form of life, the manner of existence which in your special struggle of the spirit against the flesh will emerge more clearly as your own, as the one which is intended for you, as the form of life allotted and lent to you by God.'[37] My character, the specific form of my existence, is shaped in the struggle between God's call and my physically, psychologically and socially conditioned reality – which also means a reality shaped by sin. For that reason the believer who sees himself free for fulfilment, and called to it, will look for criteria for his behaviour.

Criteria for our fulfilment

If the believer sees his own fulfilment embedded in the process of God's fulfilment, will he not anxiously ask how far he may be allowed to venture, what is still permissible for him? I am shown that I am affirmed to an unlimited degree – I may affirm myself boundlessly, including those elements in myself which I cannot really affirm. What becomes of me I leave to the one who affirms me. The fulfilment of my self is as it were its purpose and its programme. In this way, my search for criteria for my behaviour takes on a new significance: I no longer have to do this or that to arrive at a goal which I find more or less satisfactory. If God constitutes my self, I must not worry about reaching my goal. If my finding a goal is an integral part of my self-determination which is given by God and consists in God himself, then fulfilment can no longer be a problem for me. My question, then, must rather be: How can God's fulfilment be effected? How will I least get in the way of it? How can it be achieved in myself and in other men? This shift in the questioning is not simply a clumsy theological trick which ends up by arguing that man may not seek fulfilment in the way in which he desires.

It would be an extremely superficial way of understanding Christianity to claim that there can be only one way of fulfilment for believers, namely love and devotion to others; anything which does not serve other men may become stunted, and I must demonstrate its function for my fellow men if I do not want it to become stunted. Thus tacitly or even confessedly love threatens to become the great drag on fulfilment as this is understood in general terminology

73

– since the Christian may not puff himself up like a leech, to use Roger Schutz's imagery once again. The commandment to love becomes a bludgeon inexorably wielded by the super-ego under Christian influence. This cannot be in accord with the gospel, with the will of God which constitutes the human self in grace.

First of all, some psychological observations should puzzle anyone who at any time deals with the commandment to love: not everything that makes itself out to be love is in fact love. What may seem to be loving concern for our neighbour may be the working of psychological mechanisms which have nothing to do with what the gospels mean by love. To mention the most obvious: by concerning myself incessantly with other people I might be running away from myself and my own problem. By permanently allowing myself to be exploited by my partner, I need not necessarily have an incomparably good and helpful disposition; the reason might also be simply weakness and an inability to offer any resistance – which might in fact be helpful. It is equally well known that love is marvellously suitable for the exercise of mastery and the fostering of dependent relationships. Would it be quite unthinkable that I might have a tendency towards depression and simply need my fellow man as an object of my devotion to secure the balance of my own psychological make-up? The catchword 'love' is therefore an inadequate definition of the criterion for fulfilment in the Christian sense. This criterion does not lie in love, which can have many meanings, but in faith, which only has one; which concludes from the fact of what I have been given that God is not only with me, but equally wants to help my fellow-man to fulfil himself. In that case, to love this person need not necessarily mean to be preoccupied with him or her day and night, fulfil their every request, withdraw and refuse for their sake. Rather, belief in the liberation of my fellow-man and his vocation to fulfilment makes me more restrained and keeps me at a distance while remaining at his disposal. I am at his disposal; I am there, if I am used, in a natural and basic attitude of devotion. It is more important that my partner develops his gifts than that I should make him happy with mine! That does not exclude the possibility of people being led beyond this latent readiness to find their own fulfilment and ultimate realization in devotion to someone else, in an active contribution to the realization of another human life. But even this also means that we discover, affirm and develop the natural and spiritual gifts which may have been given us, just as we would wish others to do. In that case love becomes the medium of fulfilment and not its limit.

Jesus' parable about the man who went on a journey, entrusting money to his servants, has introduced into everyday language the phrase that people should 'make the most of their talents' (see Matt. 24.14ff.), and it has also become a widespread view that people need not 'hide their light under a bushel' (cf. Matt. 5.15). However, this imagery is not meant to give the Christian a good conscience once he sees his gifts being put to use, or the limelight of public attention and general approval shining upon him. Rather, it creates a certain detachment from our capacities. The point is not that we must realize ourselves as Christians by using God's good gifts and exploiting them by every possible means, offering his talents and using them in his service for the good of mankind: rather, in the language of parable, the gifts are capital which he has entrusted to us and which we need only put to work. 'Master,' said the first servant in Luke's version of the parable, when it came to the reckoning, 'your pound has earned ten': the money which you left me has multiplied

75

tenfold of its own accord (Luke 19.16). What God gives us will bring forth something of itself, will have an effect, multiply of its own accord if we do not 'bury' it, protect it and conserve it. We have simply to ask ourselves: what kind of self has been entrusted to me? What have I to look after, develop and cultivate so that it does not become atrophied? This question need not be limited to the spiritual sphere nor even to that of the church. What am I interested in? What am I good at? Is there something that I can do better than others? Where in my everyday existence might something come to life, find a foothold, take up time in such a way as to fill my life, enrich it, illuminate it, develop it and make it happy? How far am I myself cognizant and responsible for the joy which prevails in my life, for the mood in which I spend my leisure time, for the songs which are sung or whistled – or are lacking – in my home?

Of course the New Testament knows a further dimension of such giftedness and endowment: 'As each has received a gift, employ it for one another, as good stewards of God's varied grace' (I Peter 4.10). It speaks of gifts which are not, as it were, laid in our cradle, which cannot be explained by parents and grandparents. There are gifts which come to a person in his or her call to participation in God's fulfilment: the gifts of understanding and being understood, of discerning and communicating, of healing and hoping. These gifts anticipate the future of human and divine fulfilment: they register a protest against all forms of alienation, not just as an announcement, but as the dawn of a new reality. So nothing would be more absurd than to want to use these particular gifts to buttress and inflate an empirical ego out for self-assertion (I Cor. 12). Where in our life, we must ask, can anything be seen of future human and divine fulfilment? Where is something growing in me that perhaps I cannot yet fully understand, but clearly comes from the abundance of the 'manifold grace of God' and might become fruitful for me and for others? A particular way of carrying on conversations, seeing through problems, encouraging and inspiring people, discovering sore points, writing letters, organizing help, enabling joy?

Perhaps there can be an even deeper awareness of such spiritual gifts. Roger Schutz writes: 'According to the gospel, "to be oneself" means to dig down until one comes up against the irreplaceable gift which is hidden in every man. Man realizes himself in God through this unique gift, which is by no means the same in one person as another. To become still, to withdraw into the wilderness, and even if it is only once in a lifetime, to come to know this gift. . .'[38] I think it possible that there are some unique gifts, but I would not think less of the gift bestowed on me if it were like that of another, or if it were only given me for a time, for a particular period in my life, or only for a few important moments. Our problem today is less that we do not want to serve one another with the 'gift which each has received' than that we do not allow one another our rights, do not accept one another and claim one another with the gift that has been given. We might perhaps begin by presupposing in others the special gift of God which makes them out and by looking for it: in faith in the universal and saving relevance of Jesus as the Christ, in the future of the realization of God for men, we may assume that each person has been given a particular gift which he alone can convey and that each believer is supplied with a special gift through which this future is given to him in advance. Understood in this way, fulfilment does not mark off one self against another, but leads to mutual complementation and support, to a community in which give and take is possible. We do away with the tiresome law that every man on this earth must live at the expense of others by accepting it as fully as possible and implementing it as widely as possible, by daring to bear the cost that we cause our fellow man and by ourselves bearing costs on his behalf. Only the one who allows others to be there for him can be there for others. We can be there for others more, the more we allow to be present in the others who are there for us the one who in his name promises his mysterious existence beyond any conceivable future and beyond any conceivable resistance.

The counter-reality of the kingdom of God

In many conversations, in planned group sessions and chance meetings, we have an experience with a spiritual dimension. When people become open to one another, the openness itself seems to become an independent healing and inspiring power between them, to bring them together and at the same time to give them freedom. Something is realized in the midst of such mutual openness which includes the 'I', 'you' and 'we' who are involved, and yet mysteriously transcends them. Even those who are not at home in a religious tradition can experience this as grace and perhaps even feel drawn to call it that. It became clear to the first disciples who met together under the impact of the life and death of Jesus that where two or three are gathered together in his name, there he is in their midst (Matt. 18.20). For them Jesus' uncompromising sacrifice of his life for the unfulfilled men on the margin of society, held fast on the shadowy side of the world, became the basis for a new sense of living. Jesus allowed the powerful to treat his life like a cup of wine, thoughtlessly spilt, or like a piece of bread which someone carelessly breaks in order to eat. He allowed his existence to be buried away like a grain of wheat, and allowed himself to be pressed out like a grape. Together the disciples ate the bread and drank the wine in memory of the way in which Jesus had dealt with his life, and in the certainty that this way of dealing with his life was the only one that made sense and had a future. Thus it dawned on them that they themselves would go through the fire together and with him, like bread made up of many grains; that they would be trodden like wine from many grapes; that they would grow together with him to form one body. This would produce a counter-reality to the world askew in its framework, support against an atomizing which individuals might cause among their fellow-men on the pretext of 'fulfilment'. The body of Christ, from which we live and as which we live, becomes a counter-reality which can survive the downfall of mankind as it destroys itself through mutual contempt and exploitation. The future begins in the midst of the rottenness of our transitory world, as it moves towards death and destruction, a future which is the dawn of the counter-reality of successful communication and a happy life. Fulfilment in faith means to take part in this counter-reality, to engage oneself body and soul, in thought and action, in the future of what has begun with Jesus Christ. Wherever something happens in our everyday life that is connected with his fulfilment, with the coming of his kingdom, it is disclosed through his future. Its justification, its significance and its guarantee are grounded in this future – even if what we are talking about is a telephone conversation or a bank remittance.

We know only too well that much of our empirical reality contradicts the fulfilment of the body of Christ and his kingdom: in the light of the future relevance of Jesus as the Christ we may see it as something which has no future. Anything which has no connection with the fulfilment of

God is to be seen and treated as irrelevant and unimportant. Whatever I recognize in myself as unacceptable belongs to the past, and the insignificance into which it will sink, no matter how powerful an impression it may make in the present. This is expressed in paradoxical fashion in the language of the New Testament: you are 'dead' (cf. Col. 3.3; Rom. 6.11; Gal. 2.19) to sin and the law – so draw the right conclusions, regard yourselves as dead, 'kill' your members and the 'affairs of the flesh' (Col. 3.5; Rom. 8.13), do not allow a place to the transitory but fix your attention on the life that has already begun to bring you meaning and fulfilment.

The last horizon

Death inevitably represents the extreme and ultimate provocation for all fulfilment which may be understood and achieved apart from faith. For the believer, however, it appears in a new light. Fulfilment and its promise, already dawning, affects and includes our empirical self, but is not limited to that: it only reaches its final goal when it is no longer hindered in any way by our empirical self, and that means when that self no longer exists as the self that we know. Our fulfilment does not take place against the dark background of the knowledge that one day death will bring it to a lamentable, devastating end; by this point we do not have to have arrived at such an extensive and successful fulfilment of our self that we can regard it as 'complete'. True, the shadow of death is the last question and the most dangerous threat for a man's empirical self. Without doubt, acceptance of this shadow and a struggle with it will contribute to the formation of our self, but for the believer this will not be an inevitable fixation, but a last opening on to the horizon of the fulfilment of God. The fulfilment of the believer takes place in the shadow of death, and at the same time in the light of the one who has 'robbed death of its power' (II Tim. 1.10). This changes the function of death for man and his fulfilment: death first makes possible the 'perfect service of God',[39] or, in a phrase which Karl Rahner has used to describe the matter, 'becoming ends and being begins.'[40] The fact that in his earthly existence man is always 'incomplete' and remains only partially 'realized' fills the believer with hope. His authentic and ultimate reality is 'hidden with Christ in God' (Col. 3.3), and it is 'not yet evident what we shall be' (I John 3.2). As Paul puts it more precisely, we shall not be 'something', but we shall be 'always with the Lord' (I Thess. 4.17); the Lord brings about, fulfils and will be all in all (I Cor. 12.6; Eph. 1.23; cf. I Cor. 15.28).

Man is not defined by his past, whatever that may look like, nor by his present, whether that oppresses him or brings him joy. He is defined by his future, by the future which God promises and discloses to him, a future which reaches into the present and determines it, which begins to transform everyday life, to change habits, to order human relationships, to 'fulfil' time. Luther's disputation theses 'On man' (1536), which have become famous, put this in the language of scholastic theology:

Thus the man of this life is pure divine matter (*pura materia Dei*) for the life of his future form.
So also for God, creation generally, which is now subject to nothingness, is the material of its glorious future form.
And just as in the beginning earth and heaven were related to their form completed in six days, namely in their matter,
so in this life man is related to his future form, until the image of God is restored and made complete.[41]

81

The value of the human self derives from its future and not from what man may demonstrate from a psychological or sociological point of view. His value rests in the fact that he may expose himself to the creative act of God, to the call of the one who 'makes the dead living and calls into being that which is not' (Rom. 4.17). Over man and the whole of the world which surrounds him there lies the expectation of the first day of creation, the expectation of pure light in which God will ultimately realize, not just something, but his kingdom, himself. To be 'mere matter' for the word of God which transforms everything – that is the glory of all creation; to be able to know that, to give thanks for it and to pray for it, is the special privilege of man. The consequence of this for the believer is not 'You should become who you are', but 'You may be the one you are to become; today you may lay claim to your future.'

How is this dignity which comes to me from the creative word of God realized in my dealings with myself, with my specific everyday 'reality'? This perspective gives us a usefully detached view of our self, which may snap its fingers at us or also cause us concern. To put it in a phrase applied by Francis of Assisi to his body: our self as ascertained by psychology and sociology then becomes our 'brother ass', which can as it were both serve those who have been set upon by robbers and be put at the disposal of our Lord for his entry into Jerusalem.

7 *Authentic Living – Specific Examples*

'I want to be what I am.'

A remark by Christine Secunda in the
Acts of the Scillitan Martyrs

The political dimension of fulfilment

Any attempt to draw conclusions from the conception of
fulfilment and Christian existence which has been discussed so far must necessarily be very personal. That is in
the nature of things. Fulfilment in faith needs to be made
specific by the individual. But precisely because this is the
case, we again discover a political element: only the community can offer the individual the ways and means of
finding and achieving fulfilment. From this perspective,
fulfilment is a problem of human rights and their realization. The preamble to the International Covenant on Economic, Social and Cultural Rights, passed by the General
Assembly of the United Nations on 16 December 1966,
includes these words:

> Recognizing that, in accordance with the Universal Dec-
> laration of Human Rights, the ideal of free human beings
> enjoying freedom from fear and want can only be
> achieved if conditions are created whereby everyone may
> enjoy his economic, social and cultural rights, as well as
> his civil and political rights . . .

The headlines in our newspapers, or our own experiences,

83

may make us sceptical about the ideal formulated here. However, these are at any rate the basic conditions for the fulfilment of man, and in creating and improving them the believer may realize himself and his Christian existence. Besides, it becomes clear here that the 'right to freedom of thought, conscience and religion' (article 18 of the Universal Declaration of Human Rights of 1948) can in no way be a remnant from a period of human history which in principle is in the past and will soon become superfluous. Men would cease to be men if they allowed themselves to be deprived – or themselves renounced the possibility – of seeking the goal and the possibility of fulfilment through reflection, mobilizing their conscience and practising their religion.

As I see it, this points to the first political task which organized Christianity has to perform in matters of human fulfilment, at any rate in our world. It must confront any person it can reach with the possibility and the meaningfulness of the question of their own person, their own fulfilment and the dangers that stand in the way. The church should support any political or cultural initiative which allows this question to emerge and makes it more precise, whether this is by centres for psychological counselling, party politics, shaping of timetables in schools or the opportunity for holidays. Christian faith invites man not only to understand himself in the light of his previous experiences, but also to claim the relevance of Jesus as the Christ for his own life, under the promise of the gospel. If my self is promised its place, its guarantee and its future in the course of God's realization of himself, it makes sense for me to be concerned about that self. It was probably a disastrous development when over the last twenty years theological ethics narrowed and became 'social ethics', and was able to say very little about the life of the individual and his responsibility for himself. Christian faith arouses in us a longing for a successful fulfilment. It invites us not to accept given situations as such without further ado. In faith man learns to recognize and articulate his claim, that he is himself and no one else, and that he may appeal to God's mysterious concern in his support. For instance, in faith I have learnt that I do not have to get on well with everyone. For me that was a great experience and a step towards freedom. Since then I have noticed that I can recognize ties and dependencies as such, and do not confuse them with love. I attempt to unmask and reject false claims which are made as it were illegitimately on me. I may be myself. I do not have to be as others would want me to be.

At the same time, Christian faith makes one critical of anything that makes extravagant claims to heighten or even fulfil one's life. I see its second political function in this connection. Criticism should not be confused with defamation: a good holiday, success at business, happiness in love – all this can be part of a fulfilment in which God's concern can affect us. But this is possible only if phantom wishes are not fed with phantom fulfilments (say for reasons of profit); if the decision is made by an authentic self and not as a result of manipulation. Besides, it is quite possible that a rainy holiday, a professional failure or unhappy love can also help towards this fulfilment. As I write these lines, I hope that in faith I shall understand that my fulfilment does not depend e.g. on the number of books that I may produce or on good reviews of them. Of course in some way one's professional field with its demands can become the medium for fulfilment – but only the medium, and not the measure. Christian faith offers means of orientation by which a man's ego stands or falls – or does not.

The third 'political' function of faith, now also using the

word in its technical sense, consists in the fact that it summons up and liberates forces concerned to recreate as many possibilities for fulfilment for as many people as possible, within the limits of political realities. Discussion about the quality of life has shown that it is almost impossible to arrive at quantifiable standards here which are generally accepted. However, the direction in which we must work is clear. Certainly human concern for bread is the first presupposition of all fulfilment, but by itself it is not sufficient: Christianity will be concerned both for a juster distribution of bread and for the recognition that man cannot live by bread alone. Work is indeed an essential means of fulfilment, but here too the Christian has a twofold interest: work must be distributed in such a way that anyone who seeks to find fulfilment in it may do so, and working conditions must be created which make it possible for man to find fulfilment at his place of work. On the other hand, man is not just fulfilled in what he does at work and what he earns: were it generally accepted, this knowledge could make things considerably easier for the unemployed and those unable to work. Christian faith inspires us to examine social life for those points where it has vitiated, hindered and diverted human fulfilment, and provide remedies. The list of possibilities and tasks which emerge here is unending. However, one misunderstanding in particular must be removed: fulfilment does not begin where it no longer comes up against any opposition. The limit to my struggle, whether I am able to shift it or in the end have to accept it, is also the means to my fulfilment. An illness, an irrevocable loss, a fateful conflict, can all become a challenge in the light of which my self emerges and takes shape. This, too, would be a task of Christian faith: to teach how to deal usefully and creatively with limitations of this kind.

The Christian who is concerned with his own fulfilment will look critically at the way in which he deals with 'parental authority'. In the course of his growing up, he may unconsciously have adopted all kinds of attitudes which in due course prove to be more of a burden than a help. The crucial factors here are not so much our circumstances and the way in which we deal with our parents, but our coping with the fact that we have allowed our parents so much of a hand in making us what we are.[42] This situation is analyzed by American counsellor Howard Halpern, from whom I have taken the title of this section. Our parents provide an orientation, a danger or a stimulus for our fulfilment, even when they are no longer alive. That equally applies to individuals to whom we have accorded a kind of parental authority. I write this in the awareness that one day my children, too, will have to say farewell to their parents if they are to discover themselves completely.

A special danger may appear here for the Christian, for whom respect for parents is a religious duty. Not least, the fourth commandment is particularly concerned with the relationship of a person to his parents: 'Honour your father and your mother, that your days may be long in the land which the Lord your God gives you' (Ex. 20.12). Luther's interpretation of this commandment in the Little Catechism has emphasized even further the tie between 'parents' and 'children' in the context of an already existing patriarchal order:

> We are to fear and love God in such a way
> that we do not despise nor enrage
> our parents and masters,
> but hold them in reverence, serve and obey them,
> love them and value them.

This interpretation of the divine commandment seems to leave little room for detachment, critical partnership or even a sober, undramatic 'farewell'. The 'parents and masters' represent God himself. According to proverbial wisdom, 'the parents' blessing' builds 'the children's houses'. True though much of this may be, the notion may to a large degree have concealed all kinds of parental tyrannies.

However, it is only as a model for the relationship of man to God that the relationship between parents and children throws its whole weight into threatening the fulfilment of the 'children'. In that case it is always the business of the 'prodigal son' to return to the 'father'. Outside his father's house the son will be exposed only to negative influences, women of the world and doubtful friends. He will squander what the father has earned and end up among the pig food. The father may stand waiting at the gate and be prepared to kill a calf for him, but the price is return: 'serving, obeying, loving and valuing'. A late mediaeval tapestry in Marburg shows the father warmly embracing his returning son, but the son is almost swallowed up in the embrace of his powerful father . . .

Since the fourth commandment and the story of the prodigal son may have had negative effects on the fulfilment of many people, a few explanatory comments may be in place here. The fourth commandment was originally addressed to grown men, and was meant to protect the old and the ageing in the same way as the Bible seeks protection elsewhere for those in need of it, for the widows and orphans, the foreigners and those without rights. Parents are to be assigned the importance they have as those who have experience of 'living in the land', above all as those who know that 'the Lord your God' has given life and land. However, in the transition from agrarian to industrial society the possession of experience in the sense of 'know how' passed from the old to the young; and in the second respect, too, there is a critical limitation to the degree to which parents can claim authority. They can expect recognition only to the degree that they know of God's gift. The authority of God limits parental authority. If they want to understand their own development in the course of divine fulfilment, parents and children will not get in the way of each other, but will be concerned to work together to see how they can help one another to a clearer, more consistent, more appropriate realization of themselves. Nor should God's authority be wrongly understood here as the claim of a super-Father whom one will not escape in the end. When, for example, Paul speaks of 'children' of God, he means grown 'sons' and 'daughters', and 'heirs' come of age, men who claim their being from God as did Jesus, the 'Son'. We should not misunderstand the New Testament when it also seeks to express this by using the image of a little child. To become like a little child, to expect things and take them for granted, and in some cases to shriek aloud in an insistence that God's kingdom is real. The point of the biblical tradition is not that man has to become small and hateful, or that he has so to speak to accept the 'little child syndrome' if he is to be assured of God's care. Jesus' parable about the 'prodigal son' is concerned with the 'merciful father' who never ceases to hope that the son will 'come to himself' (Luke 15.17 – literal translation), and who does not write off the son, does not deny him any future, but keeps it open. Paternal authority which understands itself in the light of divine authority is not condescending but liberating; it prompts man to seek freedom from alienating dependencies, 'causes and increases' – the original sense of the term *auctoritas* – the fulfilment of the 'child'. God seeks the fulfilment of fathers and sons, of mothers and daughters. God realizes himself in the freedom which the generations find from each other and for each other, and not in unquestioned dependent relationships.

It follows from this that we have to consider the points at which we are caught up in a captivity which has become a religious tabu under our parents (and parental authorities). It is obviously an element in our fulfilment, seen in the light of God, that we should not allow ourselves to be directed by unconscious or semi-conscious mechanisms, that we should not say 'yes' when we really mean 'no'. At this point we have to venture acts of liberation – inwardly and outwardly – and practise new patterns of behaviour. The insights of transactional analysis may help us a good deal here. We have to have a 'farewell' before there can be a real reunion. So a process which leads to the maturity of 'children', and enables them to show it, also contributes to parental fulfilment and is thus in a real sense the equivalent of taking seriously – 'honouring' – father and mother.

Dealing with conflicts

Conflicts are part of life. It is unthinkable that human beings should become individuals and be involved in societies without them. Thus it is even more likely to be the case that anyone who is in search of fulfilment, who recognizes and affirms it as a gift and a task, cannot avoid conflict. It may begin with conflict in himself, with a psychological struggle in which the super-ego tries to exercise its function of control. How far may I affirm myself? How far is it permissible for me to have wishes which I cherish? Must I not condemn myself when I discover such egotistic drives within myself? And it will certainly lead to conflicts in a social setting. Who is to fulfil himself: you or I? Marriages easily become arenas for a struggle for fulfilment. *You* can have a business life, meet people; you find recognition and response; *I* can stay at home, wash nappies and cook meals, do the housework and telephone the doctor. Why not the other way round?

Fulfilment certainly does not begin when the coast is clear, when my partner (or even my super ego) permits. I found this comment in Karl Rahner: 'No one develops and unfolds as it were from a purely formal structure already existing in his being; he takes the specific elements of his life from human community, from a history, from a people, from a family, and develops them (even when they are his deepest and most personal characteristics) only within this community.' Opposition to and limitation of my fulfilment is part of the specific nature of my life. As such, it cannot vitiate my fulfilment, just as the lack of particular opposition as such cannot guarantee it. However, though this insight is correct in principle, it does not alter the fact that one person must in fact do something that he does not want to, and that the other can fulfil himself to his heart's delight, perhaps at the expense of the first. So?

The traditional 'Christian' solution, put forward especially at the Reformation, runs: I do not have to ask what I want and what I might do, but what I should do and what is useful to my fellow men. The important thing is my vocation, not my talent, and I recognize my vocation from my status. As a husband I am not called upon to bear children, and as a wife and mother my primary task is not, for example, to work as a bricklayer. Although the different functions which are distributed have different significances in the wider world and therefore also find different recognition, before God every man in his profession has the same importance and the same worth, namely to be God's instrument and collaborator for the good of man and the world in which he lives. In fact there is a knowledge of the meaningfulness of every step that I take and every action

I perform which is far above the question of success and recognition, an inner identification with the earth that I dig or the chrome that I clean, an 'understanding' with the place which at this particular moment in life happens to be my own. But of course this argument does not really help to make palatable for someone else a form of fulfilment which runs contrary to this. Even at the time of the Reformation, the weakness of this approach was recognized. How was the relationship of talent to vocation to be understood in those instances where people were called to become counsellors, princes or craftsmen? This particular point would be of especial interest today. It is increasingly less evident to which social function I am called: many people in principle have the same potentialities, and yet they cannot all use them in the same satisfactory way. What can Christianity contribute to the resolution of such conflicts?

In my experience, Christians are often shy of conflict. But it is a mistake to suppose that love for one's neighbour expresses itself above all in not becoming involved in a conflict with him. Love takes seriously the conflict, its causes, its dangers and even its chances. If God is equally concerned with me and my partner in the conflict, if God's self is to be involved in both our fulfilments, then my partner is not only fighting for himself and his interests, but also for God's concern with him. In that case I recognize in him not only the threat which he possibly represents to my empirical self and its needs, but also something of the goal which he not only has to take seriously but must also pursue in all the phases of his existence, since this life is all that he has. And the significance of this life has its place, its guarantee and its future in the movement of God's fulfilment just as much as in mine. I shall therefore try not to defend myself against his claims but to make myself the advocate of his fulfilment. Along with him I shall draw out the way in which he can find the specific meaning of his life and live in accord with it. Then we will discuss how far we restrict each other, what can be avoided, how we can make and maintain elbow room for each other and in what respect we are prepared not just to tolerate but to accept each other as a limitation.

In this process we shall develop fantasies and have ideas about each other. Perhaps money can remove some limitations. We have already touched on the problems connected with marriage: some situations which husband or wife may find oppressive can perhaps be limited to a particular time of day or even removed altogether by one partner taking a more dominant part than the other, relieving the other of certain routines. It may be possible to find a meaningful substitute for one or other deficiency in the fulfilment that is hoped for. The burden of renunciation is shared as far as possible. Honest discussion and the acceptance of firm obligations in this sphere are some of the simple means which never fail to help. In that case, the conflict as such can become a challenging and inspiring means towards our own fulfilment and that of others. Once these factors go beyond the sphere of the individual – and that may often happen – we are perhaps led into political involvement. The situation of potential conflict in which one spouse is prevented from fulfilling all his or her calling may, for example, result in the demand for more possibilities of part-time involvement – for both husband and wife!

It may be possible to wrest all kinds of meaning from conflict, but for most people it will never be a pleasure to live in conflict. We cannot exclude the possibility that a conflict ceases to engage one partner or the other, and that in the interest of perceiving their true selves, indeed the selves which God wills them to fulfil, they have to part company; that colleagues bid farewell to one another; that sons and daughters leave their parents in more than a superficial sense. Here the believer recognizes the mark of this world, the mark of 'sin', about which he speaks only because he knows that the future will not belong to it. Different though the ways may have to be, all fulfilment ends in the common movement of God's self-realization.

Such an assurance cannot just be adopted in theory. Christian insights may have contacts with humanistic understanding, but Christianity does not derive its force from rational argument. It is not a programme in search of supporters but an invitation to the fullness of life. Its contents will be understood only by those who follow them, and not by those who are simply readers.

Perceiving, thanking and celebrating

Christianity cannot develop its intrinsic power to disclose and change reality as long as it is understood wrongly as an idea, an intellectual construction, a perspective on the world. Of course it also sees itself as an offer of meaning, but the meaning which is offered here transcends by far the realm of theoretical affirmation and acceptance. It is not realized in taking over a particular view of the world but in living with this view of the world – as a result of this, the theory of belief will then go on to change. Perhaps it is the fault of academic theology that the impression has arisen that faith is a theory which has to be translated into practice, and that the coherence of the theory is more important than the practice, in which it is always necessary to make qualifications. But Christianity does not live by its theory. Rather, in faith a power of life is experienced; 'grace and help, teaching and consolation are received', as a traditional liturgical phrase has it. We celebrate our liturgies

94

in the name of God, who wills to be there for us in a way beyond our control and as sheer mystery beyond all the future and through all opposition; in the name of Jesus, who in sacrificing his existence becomes relevant for us and for all existence as the Christ; and in the name of the Spirit, who teaches us to live in the light of God's concern for us, to let the relevance of Jesus Christ apply to us and to lay to claim to him. Here the empirical world begins to totter; here consolation grows in the midst of comfortlessness; confidence in the midst of obscurity and hindrance; hope in the face of death. Here sin loses its power; here the real self experiences itself as a gift in the midst of the structures of our empirical selfhood; here the new man and the new community, the body of Christ, are constituted. Here I learn to live by joining in the movement of God's fulfilment which creates my selfhood and sets it in motion; here I take bold steps into freedom and the future; here the new community of successful communication begins to grow.

In most cases it is not possible to recognize so-called practising Christians even by their Sunday visit to church. But to go to a service or to hold one only makes sense if it is a way towards human fulfilment, if there we can experience clearly the beginnings of the way in which God's fulfilment of himself takes the burden from our empirical self, leads beyond itself and makes possible confident, successful action and communication. Liturgy which does not serve human fulfilment understood in this way, is meaningless and will die. Not because people will stay away, but because God will provide no justification for it.

If it means to become aware of itself, Christian faith will always be directed towards three elements which formally also characterize traditional liturgy: time, testimony and communion. Anyone who wants to find fulfilment as Christianity really understands it first of all needs time:

not time to do something, but time to do nothing. Karl Jaspers calls freedom apparently to do nothing 'the source of everything essential'.[43] To have time not simply to flow over us but to divide and to distribute, to be able to 'take time', is surely one of the great cultural achievements of humanity: the animal is at the mercy of time. Man may take time for himself to rest and celebrate; he is not condemned to surrender helplessly to the needs of his organism, incessantly to work for the security of his existence, and to regard inevitable pauses simple as preparation for a further securing of his existence. For this reason the Israelite regarded the sabbath as a gift of God, indeed a divine commandment: on the sabbath a man does not just rest so that he can work again next day. On the sabbath, man is free. Erich Fromm puts it in this way: 'On the Shabbat one lives as if one *has* nothing, pursuing no aim except *being*, that is, expressing one's essential powers: praying, studying, eating, drinking, singing, making love. The Shabbat is a day of joy because on that day one is fully oneself.'[44] The Christian theologian might put it rather differently: in the time which is granted to him and which he may take for himself, the believer comes to himself and becomes conscious of himself. 'Only as he gives thanks to God does man fulfil his true nature.'[45] Perhaps it is no longer possible for us to continue with regular observance of the sabbath every week, or even with the habit of daily prayer. But perhaps it is possible for us every now and then to give up a whole weekend to such dreaming, thanking and remembering, or to use some holiday towards our fulfilment, to plan a retreat. Perhaps there will also be some simple tricks we can use to avoid the grip of everyday work: a slight revision in habits of sleep or watching the television; a dog to force us to go out for a walk; a small notice which even in the midst of a busy home can turn our room into a cell for a little while: Please do not disturb. The second element which the believer needs if he is to become aware of his new and real self is almost more difficult: how do I come in contact with the testimony of the movement towards God's fulfilment, of the relevance of Jesus as the Christ which reaches out towards me? Bible reading, which in past centuries was almost the be-all and end-all of evangelical piety, often leaves even the knowledgeable and the sympathetic empty and disappointed. New translations going back to the original text, or even the freshness which we can find by reading the Bible in a foreign language that we may know from holidays or business, may help to bring new significance to what is overfamiliar or incomprehensible – but who can indulge in such intellectual luxury? Television, religious broadcasts and programmes on the radio in the early morning do not impinge much on our everyday reality, where they have anything to say at all. So once again it is natural to turn to the printed word. Bible reading notes are short; at breakfast it is possible to look quickly to see if they have anything to say to us in the same way as we may look quickly at the morning paper. I know one person who has put up a tearoff calendar with texts next to his shaving mirror. Another may put a paperback in his coat to read at the bus stop. Someone else may decide to read a theological bestseller, a church paper, or to take out a subscription to a theological magazine. We shall never find and benefit from what Christianity has to contribute to our fulfilment without making some move in this direction. It is not just around in the air – we do not get it automatically from living in a world which was once shaped by Christianity.

But all this will only take on life and colour, savour and force, if we are also concerned about the third area which is necessary here: community and exchanges with others.

97

At this point the traditional form of Sunday service is just as much a failure. As a new arrival, for example, one can go to church for months, indeed join in the eucharist, without getting to know anyone. House groups and community groups may have all sorts of benefits for their members, but to outsiders they often seem to be 'closed societies'. Perhaps conferences and weekend seminars are more of a help. But maybe we should also look round for spiritual counsellors and visit them with some regularity, give them some idea of our difficulties, ask for their advice, exchange experiences of faith with them, just as the old hermits once did. Long distances and expensive journeys should not put us off. Perhaps we could become freer to talk with other people about our own interests, about our self and its fulfilment, enthuse them also to think about the same things and share their experiences and make them fruitful.

Comfort for brothers: groups and activities

By adopting the insights and practices of psychology in the professional sphere, pastoral care in the last few years has made a discovery which every believer can in fact do something about and which in my view is very closely concerned with the meaning of the gospel: being there alongside anyone who is in a crisis without making any claims on them. Presumably I am not competent enough to cure someone's illness or to heal his marriage, to remove his despair or get the better of his hopeless situation. But I can be there with him and hold him fast. I can sit with him, without any particular purpose, without any claim; I can pay attention and listen, can think through his difficulties with him and join him in looking for a way. What possibilities or needs arise here will depend on our particular occupation and perhaps on our time of life. It may sound trite, but to visit sick neighbours, to telephone lonely aunts, to have time for the disturbed are still ways in which every Christian has an opportunity to be active. Often such challenges are nearer to home than we would like, in our own family or on the floor above us. They should not give us a bad conscience: we should recognize them and see them as occasions in which we can bring about something of God's fulfilment.

It may perhaps be that a group of involved people is formed and begins an initiative with a particular social or local-political aim. Unexpected and incalculable experiences can arise in common work on a project. Among a group of colleagues I have found that individual involvement has been caught up into a greater whole in which particular contributions can no longer be distinguished, and this has been a happy way towards fulfilment.

But here everyone reacts differently: one is better in a group, another prefers to make an individual contribution; perhaps things change in the course of one's life. However it may seem in a particular situation, the important thing is that we should try to live in awareness of our wider surroundings. It alters my perspective if, for example, I know of the suffering of Christians in Ethiopia or the struggle of the churches in Latin America; if I begin to see myself as part of world Christianity. In that case I may be interested in a well which has to be drilled in Tamilnadu, or a school class in the north Brazilian diocese of Recife. I will understand my involvement in a greater whole, I will look for contacts and possibilities of participation. I will react sensitively to news which reaches me: it makes me ashamed not to be able to do more in a catastrophe than to send a contribution to Beirut or to North Africa – yet that is a sign for one's brother which God may take up

99

into the movement of his fulfilment as much as he takes me up myself.

Renunciation and suffering

The fact that renunciation and suffering have often been required and endured in past centuries at the cost of fulfilment should not make us blind to the place that they have in a fulfilment affirmed in the name of God. The man who is in a position to deal meaningfully and productively with renunciation and suffering is not the one who is sorry for himself but the one who is self-assured. It was said that Jesus was a 'glutton and a winebibber' (Matt. 11.19); at any rate, he does not seem to have been hesitant about enjoying a good meal. Yet when he saw the need, he was ready to stand fast, and even to undergo torture and die. To live in an awareness of renunciation and suffering can evidently become an act of fulfilment, a possibility of creative involvement in our own reality.

It may begin quite undramatically. In the course of the years every household accumulates a good deal of junk. That is equally true of its way of life and its domestic habits. In my everyday life I can discover patterns which are established and convenient, but which, if I am honest, I should no longer continue. I shall have brought some of them with me from my parents' home, and others will have resulted from particular circumstances connected with my work. If I am concerned with my fulfilment, it may be worth while drawing up a balance sheet every now and then and getting rid of some of the things I do not need. A move or a change of job is a good opportunity for that.

Our particular stage of life will make a difference. Generally speaking, as our society suggests to us, we are concerned for growth, development, an extension of the possibilities of life. That can easily lead to a failure to recognize in private life the point at which further development no longer makes sense, at which unlimited growth becomes a burden. For the moment we still have no culture of self-restraint, the socialization of the private at least when it no longer has any kind of private function. Roger Schutz has put forward this point of view in his second 'letter to the people of God':

> Share all that you have and you will find freedom. Resist the pressure to be a consumer: the more you buy, the more dependent you become. The beginning of injustice lies in the accumulation of savings for yourself and your children. Fair sharing presupposes that everyone has an equal value and does not create any dependence. That is true as much for the individual as for the state.
>
> It is impossible to change one's standard of life in a day. So we urgently ask families, congregations, communities and church leaders step by step, over seven years, to give up whatever is not absolutely necessary.[46]

My proposal does not aspire to the level of the ethical claim made by Roger Schutz, but it may perhaps be seen as a first 'bourgeois' step along the lines which he suggests. Material restraint could begin with wages and salaries. Whatever I may earn, I should not simply regard it as my own, either for consumption or for developing resources. I should build up a savings account, in my name, but not for my own private use. I should pay into this savings account by standing order a certain percentage of my regular income. I might begin with two per cent and in a few years increase the sum which I forgo to six, eight or ten per cent. I will use this special account for giving towards what I know to be urgent needs: that will include world crises, but also special actions in particular cases of need, sending parcels or acting as sponsor: my savings account will leave behind traces in many countries on earth. To put it in capitalist terms: I shall invest sensibly; to put it in Christian terms: at least to some extent I shall do what is expected of me. For some years there has been talk, at least in the church papers, of 'Mr Ten per Cent': he is prepared to give away ten per cent of his net income for 'bread for the world' if he finds a particular number of people prepared to do the same thing. A further step in renunciation might be not to reserve the right to dispose of money saved in this way, and not even to have a say in giving help. On the other hand, one's own deliberate sending of certain sums makes clear an involvement in particular situations of need. A rule for the early Christian community was that people should let coins 'sweat in the hand' until they knew to whom to give them. However I may organize my renunciation, it will always become a way of realizing my fulfilment.

The financial aspect of renunciation is surely the easiest. Those who do not have to worry about their fulfilment, those who begin from gaining life as the gospel promises, discover a capacity for further and perhaps more difficult forms of renunciation. They will perhaps learn to tolerate being misunderstood, being one wheel among many, failing in initiatives at one point or another, and not having ideas accepted. They may be able to tolerate not being regarded by their neighbours as what they are or may want to be. They will feel solidarity with the countless people among the by now four thousand million inhabitants of the earth who do not achieve anything, who realize no ideals, who have to occupy their tiny place and can only give a hollow laugh when they hear the word 'fulfilment' – if they understand it at all – but who hunger and thirst for righteousness and according to Jesus' promise will be filled.

Thus a fulfilment which at the same time embraces renunciation will become involved in unheard-of tension: to offer everything and yet not allow oneself to be disheartened by failure; to put forward the highest claims for oneself and one's fellow men and yet at the same time be able to live without putting them into practice; to have ideals and to fight for them, and on the other hand not to be dependent on their fulfilment. Paul put this in his own way: 'As servants of God we commend ourselves in every way . . . as unknown, and yet well known; as dying, and behold we live . . . as having nothing, and yet possessing everything' (II Cor. 6.4ff.).

Spiritual diary

It is impossible to live in full awareness without looking back, checking up and criticizing. The end of a year usually prompts us to look back on what has happened; in earlier times people used to take account at the end of each day. In penance Christians not only recalled in general terms that we are all sinners, but took reckoning of good and evil by means of a fixed schedule. Rightly understood, this could perform an important function for human fulfilment: Luther took such self-examination for granted. His advice about criteria in the Little Catechism was:

> Consider your status in accordance with the ten
> commandments,
> whether you are father, mother, son or daughter,
> in what profession and calling you are engaged,
> whether you are disobedient, unfaithful, lazy,
> angry, undisciplined, quarrelsome,
> whether you have done anyone wrong
> in word or deed,
> whether you have stolen, been neglectful or done harm.

Models for penance following individual commandments can be found in our hymn books; Ignatius Loyola even expected a written account of individual sins of which the believer was aware. Of course such practices can be misused. But they are not intended to make a man seem insignificant and hateful to himself and his fellows; they are intended to help him to clarify and cope with his everyday experience and behaviour, to free him for new action. In its traditional form penance is probably no longer a helpful institution, accessible to anyone, but those who know in faith that their fulfilment has its place and its guarantee in the context of God's own fulfilment will appreciate its purpose. I have taken over for my own private use a custom which we have followed by our children's bedsides, namely at the end of the day to ask, 'What was good today?' 'What was important?' 'What was not good?' Finally, one means of remaining aware and considering one's experience which has gone out of fashion, but is still very effective, is to keep a diary. Those who are fond of using pen and paper will discover that a diary can become an instrument for living in an almost technical sense. I hold on to what preoccupies me, what I am concerned with; by writing it down I admit it to myself and at the same time assign it a place: an important sentence which I have read, a question which has been raised by some political news; memorable remarks which our children have made, an important theme raised by yesterday evening's visit. In my diary I prepare for difficult conversations, look for grounds for failure and disappointment, take up stimuli from everyday life, go into questions of belief.

25 December. How could Christmas influence and change the coming weeks? Other standards: crib, stable – more freedom in everyday life, less identification with my profession and its system of points . . . Children and angels are what it's about. Look systematically for children and angels. W/M, Peter, H group – what must I ask them?

See mankind qualified by the coming of Jesus!

31 December. Today the sexton said that they won't now find the body of the suicide in the canal because of all the ice. How many people died over this Christmas? How many disappointed hopes does Christianity already have on its conscience?

4 January. When do our children have a really successful day? In the last resort are their standards different from those of adults?

7 January. Departure of Dr S for Tanzania. Longing for vocation and mission. Am I fooling myself when I say that I would seriously try. . .

14 January. Ss here yesterday. He: not to allow oneself to be devoured by one's own best intentions. She: fill the area of theology: the rich farmer – you fool?

24 January. Harald, six years old, refuses to play with four-year-old Claudia. 'I don't play with girls.' She retorts: 'I'm not a girl, I'm Claudia.'

27 January. Today in the clinic: FW and Frau M – the two types of illness. How much one remains 'outside' as a healthy person! And early today, Luke 4.

Lüneburg – Rats-Apotheke: *Neque herba neque malagma*

sanavit eos, sed tuus, Domine, sermo – neither herb nor plaster cured them, but thy word, O Lord.

Prayer and meditation

The diary in which I not only collect together superficial happenings but also write down my existence with its longings and its gratitude, its inner concern and deep expectation, can easily become a prayer book. Conscious living has an inner tendency towards prayer. The experience of the moment turns into language and thanksgiving. I am thinking of a passage in Christa Wolf's book *Divided Heaven*:

> The white snowflakes stood out sharply on the brown soil. Tomorrow the first warmer wind from the West would break up all the contours and produce new, harsher ones . . . Rita laughed. How she knew everything! As though it were a part of her! Thanks for every bird song, she thought, for the cool flowing water, for the morning sun and the shadow of the trees in summer.[47]

A frequent objection to prayer is that it is no more than a conversation with oneself. And even if that were the case, the conversations one has with oneself can be extremely important, both personally and for others. Conversation with myself prevents me from accumulating my own experience so that it becomes a short circuit between attraction and reaction. In conversation with myself I reflect on the distance between myself and the empirical reality which surrounds me. I take a step back, I become aware, I 'reflect' my experience and my behaviour. Conversation with myself makes me aware of something that otherwise I sense only dimly; it helps me to identify and to clarify, to articulate wishes and make plans specific. At one time, for many men prayer offered the great institutionalized possibility of talking with themselves; in this respect too, nothing can make good its loss. From a formal point of view, prayer often takes the form of a fictitious conversation or, even more frequently, of an address directed to an intangible 'you'. I put myself in the wider context of my reality, I allow myself to address the people in whose midst I live; the past, from which I come, and the future, about which I am uncertain. To this degree prayer is not something specifically Christian: prayer is a human activity, the means and expression of human fulfilment. Christian prayer addresses as 'Father' the 'You' who in a completely mysterious way, beyond our control, is concerned to be there for us for all time and despite all resistance it gives the title 'Lord' to Jesus, whose utter saving and universal relevance I may accept for myself, for all men and all beings. The believer knows that he cannot expose himself and entrust himself, in his own strength, to this being who is beyond his control, this relevance of the one who is relevant *par excellence*. His prayer is offered 'in the Spirit'. In prayer, the one who prays is caught up in the movement of the God who fulfils himself. It becomes clear to him within what terms of reference the empirical self can claim understanding, where it gets in the way of its own programme and the selfhood of others. Prayer anticipates God's future, consoling and inspiring.

Although prayer is so urgent a human need, many people know only a caricature of it, seeing it as a request to 'someone' for 'something'. God is not 'someone' and we do not ask him for 'something'. His commandment forbids us to imagine him as 'someone', and his goodness is too great for us ultimately to imagine that any 'thing' could be more important than himself. Meditation as it is practised in

Eastern religions, which is also by no means alien to the Christian tradition, can help us to open up the 'I-thou' model of prayer, which pietism has made too narrow, and perhaps to disclose prayer again to more people.

Almost by chance (though Lessing said that the word 'chance' was blasphemy), I came across the practice of meditation in a monastery. It is beginning to break up something which in retrospect I now see as a danger of rigidity in my thinking, to make it flow and involve it in easy movement. I am beginning to find a new way of dealing with pictures, words, observations, biblical statements. I find myself in a wider setting. Each person will find his or her own way of entering this setting, breathing its atmosphere and experiencing the most wonderful encounters within it:

> You come, a ship full laden, enter the harbour of this day and discharge your load. Lie alongside, make fast and I will take over your cargo! You ancient freighter, come, storm-tossed and battered and yet still seaworthy, you ark of all good things!

> Let me billow out like a sail, rather than lying tightly furled, when the wind begins to rise; not rolled up and made fast, but catching the wind with all my being, at the same time taut to what must be carried along: profession, family, the people who meet me today. I would not flap in the wind like a flag, but be filled with you, who drive me along above the waves – you are the storm, you are the wave and you are also the harbour!

> I hold myself out to you. I would expose myself to your life-giving strength, I believe in you. You are Lord and make alive, just as all the plants in the garden expose

themselves to the wind each in its own way: the cherry tree in a different way from the rose hedge and the rose hedge in a different way from the grass. So help me to respond to your life-giving strength, to allow myself to be grasped by you without resistance.

Let me be driven like a cloud before you, who give clouds, air and winds their course. Let me be driven by you as I go on my way, as I speak and listen and write and frame my words. You know where they will fall, and where they can give the rain. . .

And Now?

Some books are as much use as the information that they have conveyed; others are as much use as the index with which it is possible to find one's way around them. Yet others can take on a renewed life when one has turned the last page.

When I have read this last kind of book, perhaps I go once again through the markings I have made, complete my notes on the last page or wherever else I have found room to write them, make a private index with explicit references to particular points, and the pages on which they appear. That is probably the way of someone who has a good deal to do with books.

As soon as I have the opportunity, I then literally try to get out into the open. I go for a walk, by myself, on a route which I know, so that I do not have to think about it, and I choose it so that no one will disturb me. It is said of the old hermits and desert fathers that they often wandered round their cells to collect their thoughts and rid themselves of all distractions. As we walk silently, this thing or that falls away, and a good deal of our thinking sorts itself out. Reading a book which appeals to us always arouses feelings, recollections, longings. It opens up clefts and buried shafts into that hidden realm of what we have always wanted, thought, hoped for and perhaps even feared. As we sort out our impressions, a whole variety of different voices may be heard from the more distant or closer past, shrill or comfortingly present. I need not close myself to all of them; I can listen to them and assign them a place.

The diary I have mentioned can help me, as can a letter or a conversation. Now I may tell a close friend about what I have read and the impression it has had on me; perhaps I will read a few passages out aloud. What do you think of that? Is it really true? I don't understand it – what can it mean? And the most important question: I had an idea ... what do *you* think?

I lend the book, slip it to someone who may be interested, give it as a present – in the hope of some conversation about it. Perhaps I also search in things that I have read at other times for something along the same lines, or even contradictory. Throughout this process, what I have read becomes digested more and more until only a few characteristic phrases, only a few theoretical notions remain in my memory to form as it were a grip and a handle by which I can grasp and hand on its important contents.

By this time it has usually emerged what I should now go on to do – in theory, through a walk round a bookshop, or by the announcement of a particular seminar; or in practice, by a call to friends, planning an evening together or sharing in a project. Of course civic or communal initiatives cannot simply grow out of reading a book. Yet this is evidently a sore point for many of us. Must it always be that it is easier for us to go to church on Sunday than to write a letter to the local authority?

Many factors combine to produce specific results from what we have read: by then the individual points which prompted us may have been forgotten. What we read, hear, perceive and then say or write down contributes its own impulses to the process of our life. We cannot set this process in motion nor can we guarantee its success; nor need we do so. We are empowered to understand it and to accomplish it in the saving power of the one who bears that name which is so circumstantial and yet so promising: 'I will be there for you as the one who will be there for you.' The old Hebrew name for God could perhaps be dismissed as a meaningless linguistic curiosity, had not Jesus Christ shown in his living, suffering and dying what it means to claim this name for himself and others and thus to open up the future. By him I find myself set between the beginning and the goal of my own reality and that of the whole world, between alpha and omega. I hear him say, 'Because I live, you will live also' (John 14.19). I see myself and all who hear those words invited to venture the answer, 'I live – I am who I am!'

Notes

1. Roger Schutz, *Vivre l'inespéré*, Les Presses de Taizé, 1966.

2. Johann Wolfgang von Goethe, 'Urworte, Orphisch', *Sämtliche Gedichte* I, Gedenkausgabe vol. I, Zurich 1950, p. 523.

3. Augusto Monterroso, 'Der Frosch, der ein richtiger Frosch sein wollte', *Kurzprosa*, Leipzig 1977, p. 37.

4. Rainer Maria Rilke, from the *Stundenbuch* (*Book of Hours*), 1905.

5. Dorothee Sölle, *Die Hinreise. Zur religiösen Erfahrung. Texte und Überlegungen*, Stuttgart 1975, pp. 165ff.; id., *Das Recht, ein anderer zu werden. Theologische Texte*, Sammlung Luchterhand 43, 1971.

6. Hermann Hesse, 'Klein and Wagner' in *Klingsor's Last Summer*, Cape 1971, pp. 73, 74, 90, 96, 139.

7. *Studientexte zur marxistisch-leninistischen Ethik*, edited by the Forschungsgruppe Ethik der Pädagogischen Hochschule 'Karl Liebknecht', under the direction of Günter Junghänel and Sigrid Tackmann, Berlin 1976, pp. 157, 150.

8. P. E. Krjazev, 'Persönlichkeitsbildung als sozialer Prozess', in *Die Personlichkeit im Sozialismus*, Berlin 1972, pp. 37ff. (46, 49).

9. Erich Fromm, *To Have or to Be?*, Cape 1978, pp. 77, 141, 170–2, 202.

10. I have in mind here the writings of Kurt Goldstein, Carl Rogers, Viktor Frankl, Karen Horney, Abraham Maslow and Charlotte Bühler (see also the next note).

11. Charlotte Bühler, *Wenn das Leben gelingen soll. Psychologische Studien über Lebenserwartungen und Lebensergebnisse*, Munich/Zurich 1969, p. 50; id., *Psychologie im Leben unserer Zeit*, Special edition Munich/Zurich 1962; cf. also C. Bühler and M. Allen, *Introduction to Humanistic Psychology*, Monterey, Calif. 1973, pp. 45f.

12. Friedrich Nietzsche, *The Antichrist*, Penguin Books 1969, pp. 117, 131.

13. Quoted from Walter Künneth, *Antwort auf den Mythus. Die Entscheidung zwischen dem nordischen Mythus und dem biblischen Christus*, Berlin 1935, p. 128.

14. Karlheinz Deschner, *Das Kreuz mit der Kirche. Eine Sexualgeschichte des Christentums*, Düsseldorf and Vienna ²1974, pp. 382, 389, 95.

15. Plato, *Gorgias 492E*, quoting Euripides.

16. W. F. Arndt, F. W. Gingrich and W. Bauer, *A Greek-English Lexicon of the New Testament*, University of Chicago Press 1957, p. 80.

17. Dietrich Bonhoeffer, *The Cost of Discipleship*, SCM Press 1959, pp. 77f.

18. Ibid., p. 85.

19. The text comes from *Annotationes in aliquot capita Matthaei*, 1531, on Matt. 16.24f.; cf. *J. Calvins Auslegung der Evangelienharmonie*, ed. H. Stadtland-Neumann and G. Vogelbusch, II, Neukirchen-Vluyn 1974, pp. 70f., also on Matt. 16.24: 'We should be prepared to become nothing, so that God can live and rule in us alone.'

20. Jodocus van Lodensteyn, quoted from O. Weber and E. Beyreuther, *Die Stimme der Stillen. Ein Buch zur Besinnung aus dem Zeugnis von Pietismus und Erweckungsbewegung*, Stuttgart n.d., p. 57, on Matt. 8.34.

21. *Franz von Assisi. Geliebte Armut. Texte vom und über den Poverello*, edited by Gertrude and Thomas Sartory, Freiburg im Breisgau 1977, p. 62.

22. Klaus Thomas, *Handbuch der Selbstmordverhütung. Psychopathologie, Psychologie und Religionspsychologie einschliesslich der Eheberatung und Telefonseelsorge*, Stuttgart 1964, pp. 304ff.

23. Tilmann Moser, *Gottesvergiftung*, Frankfurt am Main 1976, pp. 14, 36.

24. Seward Hiltner, *Theological Dynamics*, Abingdon Press 1975.

25. Friedrich Nietzsche, *Human, All Too Human*, ch. 137 in *Works* ed. O. Levy, Foulis, Edinburgh 1909, vol. VI, p. 146.

26. Karl Barth, *Church Dogmatics* III, 2, T. & T. Clark 1960, pp. 132, 133f., 160.

27. Martin Luther, *Kritische Gesamtausgabe*, Weimar 1883ff. (=WA), 10, 1/1, 72, 12; 37, 234, 33.

28. Quoted from *Thema Gott. Frage von gestern und morgen*, edited by Rolf Baumann and Hellmut Haug, Stuttgart 1970, p. 35.

29. Thomas Aquinas, *Summas theologica* I, II, 4, 3 and 1.

30. Martin Luther, WA 5, 175.

31. Quoted from Reinhold Weier, *Das Thema vom verborgenen Gott von Nikolaus von Kues zu Martin Luther*, Münster im Westfalen 1967, p. 172 n.5.

32. Meister Eckhart, *Deutsche Predigten und Traktate*, ed. Josef Quint, Munich ⁴1977, pp. 325f.

33. Dorothee Sölle, *Phantasie und Gehorsam. Überlegungen zu einer künftigen christlichen Ethik*, Stuttgart/Berlin ²1968, p. 63.

34. Martin Luther, WA 17, II, 243.

35. Martin Luther, WA 23, 156, 30ff.

36. Quoted from K. Friz, *Stimme der Ostkirche*, Stuttgart 1950, pp. 86f.

37. *Church Dogmatics* III, 4, T. & T. Clark 1961, p. 388. Cf. Karl Rahner, *Foundations of Christian Faith*, Darton, Longman and Todd 1978, pp. 308f.: 'By the fact that a person finds God, that he falls, as it were, into the absolute, infinite and incomprehensible abyss of all being, he himself is not consumed into universality, but rather he becomes for the first time someone absolutely unique. This is so because it is only in this way that he has a unique relationship to God in which this God is *his* God.'

38. Roger Schutz, *Vivre l'inespéré*.

39. Paul Althaus, *Die christliche Wahrheit. Lehrbuch der Dogmatik*, Gütersloh ⁵1959, p. 413.

40. Cf. Karl Rahner, *Foundations of Christian Faith*, p. 272.

41. The text follows the edition by Gerhard Ebeling, *Disputatio de Homine. Text und Traditionshintergrund*, Tübingen 1977, p. 23.

42. Howard Halpern, *Cutting Loose. A Guide to Adult Relationships with Your Parents*, Simon and Schuster 1977.

43. Karl Jaspers, *Philosophische Autobiographie*, new edition, Munich 1977, p. 63.

44. Erich Fromm, *To Have or to Be?*, p. 57.

45. Karl Barth, *Church Dogmatics* III, 2, p. 171.

46. Roger Schutz, *Vivre l'inespéré*.

47. Christa Wolf, *Der geteilte Himmel*, dtv 915, 1973, pp. 21f.